Cast Iron Decoration

E. Graeme Robertson and Joan Robertson

Cast Iron Decoration

A WORLD SURVEY

WHITNEY LIBRARY OF DESIGN an imprint of
WATSON-GUPTILL PUBLICATIONS/NEW YORK

First published in the United States in 1977 by the Whitney Library of Design,
an imprint of Watson-Guptill Publications,
a division of Billboard Publications, Inc.,
1515 Broadway, New York, New York 10036

Copyright © 1977 by Joan Robertson
First published 1977 in Great Britain

Manufactured in Great Britain

Library of Congress Cataloging in Publication Data

Robertson, Graeme.
  Cast iron decoration.

  Bibliography: p.
  Includes index.
    1. Architectural ironwork.   I. Robertson, Joan,
joint author.   II. Title.
NA3950.R6   739'.47   76-27355
ISBN 0-8230-7122-7

Contents

Foreword

In 1957 one of us spoke on cast iron ornamentation to the National Gallery Society of Victoria. The Chairman of Trustees of the Gallery said the next morning: 'It is very curious. Overnight they have been hanging that ironwork you were talking about all over Melbourne.' We see but we do not perceive.

Indeed, cities may be perceived in many ways, as may the component buildings. To see the whole, as is so often done, means neglecting details, while seeing parts adds interest to the whole. To become interested in one facet creates a sense of intimacy which the whole does not evoke, yet it is necessary to observe the setting as well. An interest in cast iron ornamentation enlivens a walk through many cities, and, indeed, leads to wandering in parts of cities which would otherwise not be visited. Ironwork is usually unnoticed by the passer-by, yet, when interest is aroused, a city almost magically acquires a new and fascinating aspect. The patterns vary more than the arrangement, but this too varies from city to city.

Our interest began with the realization that cast iron in our own city of Melbourne was being heedlessly torn off houses, and as often as not replaced by unsympathetic materials. The vandalism went unrecognized, and some builders were undoubtedly adept at convincing householders of the desirability of getting rid of the old-fashioned material. Paradoxically the lapse of a century is often necessary to remove that stigma. The greater menace of wholesale demolition of houses was to come later: the efforts of developers were even considered laudable until recently, when the forces of conservation were mobilized.

At all events it was not realized that Melbourne's main claim to architectural distinctiveness lay in its cast iron ornamentation. It seemed obvious that an attempt should be made to change the attitude of the community to the treasures it possessed as a Victorian city built up in the Victorian era. This resulted in the publication of *Victorian Heritage* in 1960.

Thus began a trail which has been followed by us in Australia and elsewhere in the world. We quickly discovered that Australia was not alone in its failure to notice its cast iron ornamentation. Although part of architecture, cast iron finds little place in books on architecture, nor is the present-day architect concerned with it unless he is historically minded. Yet for more than a century it was fashionable and widely used by builders and architects. Now, as it is acquiring sufficient age to gain the sanction of being historical, it has to withstand modern

7

economical conditions to survive. In city centres where the old buildings provide less accommodation and less financial return than their modern tall counterpart, they are replaced. This is inevitable, but regrettable, for iron decoration is not lacking in aesthetic qualities and the houses were more graceful, better built, more durable and quieter than most of the replacements. Decoration with cast iron is seemingly not consistent with present-day architecture. But if cast iron is of the past, as a reminder of a more graceful past let it survive. Before it is too late the forces of preservation need to be stimulated, otherwise some cities will lose the only architectural distinction they possess, and will be much poorer for the loss. Tradition is rooted in buildings, for they are a visible and tangible reminder of history. Architecture itself is a form of art in which all may participate, and, since much of our lives is spent within its walls it has a unique importance. Retention of what is worthy promotes a sense of stability. This may penetrate deeply into the psychology of the people, favouring the lasting rather than the ephemeral.

Decoration is satisfying if it aesthetically complements the architecture, and serves a useful function. It directs attention to the house which it adorns, and often to the whole street as well.

This book deals chiefly with a homely aspect of architecture. Houses show the influence of the men who designed them, and of the centuries which have gone before. They may reveal man's desire for ornament, restrained or flamboyant.

It is necessary to define the scope of this book, since limitation is compulsory when the subject is so vast. An attempt has been made to select the common type of cast iron ornamentation in the cities depicted, especially that which distinguishes one city from another, but intriguing contacts between cities and even between countries (Scottish and Australian patterns found in Beirut, for instance) will also be noted. It is regretted that the description of cast iron ornamentation rarely extends beyond major cities; further, it has not been possible to visit all cities bearing cast iron decoration, or to include all visited. Many places have little or no cast iron, or show no new principles of usage. In most parts of the world it was difficult, or impossible, to obtain information in advance about the usage of cast iron. New Orleans is a notable exception; and we have an intimate knowledge of Australian usage, which in its extent and diversity is without parallel in the world. Australian cities grew up during the cast iron era, and their climate – calling for verandas and balconies for outdoor living – led to a spectacular flowering of ornamental ironwork.

This work deals chiefly with ornamental (not structural) cast iron used in an architectural context. Only passing attention will be paid to prefabricated iron buildings or façades. Fortunately during the last few years in New York the Friends of Cast-Iron Architecture have made an intensive study of complete façades and buildings made of cast iron (see pp. 37–38).

Cast iron flourished later than wrought iron (chiefly from the end of the eighteenth century) and, while the latter has a voluminous literature, little has been written about cast iron despite its extensive use in architecture (see the bibliography, below).

Because photography can be selective it is admirably adapted to show details of construction and reveal the beauty which may be found in unlikely places. This work is largely a photographic essay on the forms taken by cast iron ornamentation, its national variations, its relationship to architecture, and its contribution to

8

the attractiveness of buildings. The photographs have been taken over many years, and unfortunately many buildings shown will have been demolished since they were photographed.

It is impossible to thank all those who have helped in the preparation of this book. Not least are those who, by their friendship and companionship, have made our stay in their cities enjoyable. Amongst these are Dr and Mrs Denis Brinton in London, Professor and Mrs D. E. Denny-Brown in Boston, Dr and Mrs Dean Echols in New Orleans, and Dr and Mrs Eddie Bharucha in Bombay.

Dr M. S. Higgs of the Edinburgh School of Architecture made possible the solution of riddles posed by Corio Villa in Geelong, Australia, by recognizing the similarity between an illustration in *Victorian Heritage* and a drawing in a publication of the foundry of Charles D. Young of Edinburgh. The excitement of the trail which followed is unmatched in our experience.

We are deeply indebted to our old friend, and admirer of Australia, Mr William Pain of New York for sharing his enthusiasm and intimate knowledge of his own city. Exploring New York with him was a great joy. A more recent friend (by correspondence only) is Margot Gayle, chairman of the Friends of Cast-Iron Architecture in New York. The introduction was effected by *Ornamental Cast Iron in Melbourne*, and resulted in a much appreciated Honorary Membership of the Friends. She has been responsible for the recent upsurge of interest in the previously unrecognized wealth of complete cast iron buildings and façades in Manhattan, New York.

Dr Leon Whitsell provided invaluable help in San Francisco and Columbia, California, as well as including us in his happy family life. Dr Earl Walker acted as mentor and guide in Baltimore. Dr Almeido Lima introduced us to Eiffel's lift in Lisbon and Dr Luis Saénz Arroyo to the Moorish pavilion in Mexico City. Sr Arq. Eliseo Arredondo González of Mexico City, introduced by Mrs D. Nairn, provided the interesting history of this fascinating portable building.

In Australia, Dr Kenneth Jamieson was a very agreeable and helpful companion in Brisbane, while in Adelaide Dr R. Rischbieth joined enthusiastically in midnight hunts for cast iron in his city, when the empty streets facilitated search. Dr and Mrs C. Craig in Tasmania and Mr Kevin Fahy in Sydney were very helpful. Mr Archie Forwood gave us the invaluable catalogue of the Adelaide iron foundry owned by his progenitor. The value of this will be realized in the chapter on Adelaide. The illustrations for plate 334 and figures 8–10 were printed from the copper plates made for the 1901 Melbourne catalogue of William Stephens's Excelsior Foundry. These were very generously exchanged by the late Mr William Stephens Tregellas, grandson of the original William Stephens, for a copy of *Victorian Heritage*. Recently Mrs Tregellas found a box full of zinc half-tone plates which may, when cleaned, add to our knowledge of the early foundry. We are particularly grateful to the Stephens Tregellas dynasty.

The National Trust of Australia (Victoria), and in particular its chairman, Mr Rodney Davidson, have given unstinting assistance. It is also pleasant to have this opportunity to thank the staffs of the La Trobe Library, State Library of Victoria, and the Baillieu Library, University of Melbourne, and especially Miss Patricia Reynolds and Miss Mary Lugton for their untiring interest and assistance. Without exception those who were kind enough to help in the search became excited by the material and have been left with an abiding interest in the ornamentation.

The trail still continues. Four books have been published or are in preparation for an Inner Suburban Series for the National Trust of Australia (Victoria) and much material has been collected for a museum which the National Trust intends to establish. What more suitable place for a museum could be found than Melbourne, which has more cast iron ornamentation of houses than any other city in the world?

Melbourne

E.G.R. and J.R.

1 Introduction

The material

It seems customary to refer to all decorative iron as wrought iron, although the latter forms but a small proportion of that used in architecture during the nineteenth century. A brief description of the material and its manufacture would thus seem helpful.

A few artifacts provide evidence that casting was practised in England as early as the fifteenth century. Founders (as distinct from smiths) had originally been concerned only with brass and copper castings, but later they extended their interest to iron as well, and in 1532, during the reign of Henry VIII, the Worshipful Company of Founders erected its first hall in London The earliest forms of castings were firebacks, grave slabs, cannons, cannon-balls and cooking utensils.

However, the necessity of their condition imposed many limitations upon the early founders. Charcoal, the fuel used for smelting, was easily crushed by the heavy iron ore. The volume of the charge in the furnace was thus limited, and the iron was incompletely molten because of the difficulty of obtaining a sufficiently high temperature. Further, so great was the destruction of trees that it became impossible to obtain adequate supplies of charcoal. About 1713, at Coalbrookdale in Shropshire, the ironmaster Abraham Darby discovered a successful method of using coke produced from coal, with which England was so plentifully supplied. Improved methods of blowing air into the mixture of iron ore and coke in the blast furnace to speed combustion also played an important part in revolutionizing the technique of smelting. These methods paved the way for the Industrial Revolution, with its enormous demand for casting in the manufacture of machinery, and later for fences and balconies of the innumerable terraces of new houses built during the last century.

In smelting, iron ore is placed between many layers of coke and fired in a furnace, assisted by blowing air into the bottom of the furnace. Thus an intense heat is attained and eventually molten iron runs from the bottom of the blast furnace into moulds, or, more commonly, into a channel with bilateral side branches. The fanciful resemblance to a sow feeding her litter is responsible for the broken-off components being called pig-iron. The bars of pig-iron may be conveniently transported for further working, and are used as a basis for producing cast iron, wrought iron, and steel, each having different properties and usages.

Cast iron contains 5–8 per cent of impurities, the chief of which is carbon (3·5–4·25 per cent). The impurities cause it to become liquid when sufficiently heated, so that it can be cast in moulds. In the manufacture of castings an initial pattern is carved in close-grained wood. In the traditional process of multiplication two 'boxes' are used. These are rectangular frames without top or bottom which are filled with fresh sand in which clay acts as a binding material. The sand is firmed by ramming and the upper surfaces are smoothed and covered by powdered graphite, which facilitates the later separation of the boxes. The pattern is then depressed into the upper surface of one box (called the drag). The other box (the cope) is turned over and lowered on to the drag so that the pins on the sides of the drag fit into eyelets on the cope, thus securing accurate register. The sand of the cope is rammed down to surround the pattern. The cope is next lifted, and the pattern removed. The depressions made by the pattern in cope and drag are smoothed and sprinkled with graphite, and the cope is replaced on top of the drag. Communicating channels now represent the pattern, and into these molten metal is poured through a hole previously made in the sand of the cope, while gases are expelled through other holes. The metal is allowed to cool, the cope is raised, and the casting is lifted from its bed. Irregularities in the casting are removed by filing.

The making of hollow columns involves the use of a core of rough rope covered with sand and graphite. The core is suspended so that it comes to lie within the mould of the column when the boxes are brought together. Molten iron is then run into the resulting cylindrical space.

The heat of the molten iron destroys the binding clay in the 'green' sand, hence before the next casting is made the adhesive qualities must be restored by adding fresh clay. Once the process has been started many castings may be made, reproducing the shape of the pattern. The iron castings may themselves be used as patterns, but the final result will be slightly smaller, because of contraction during cooling. This ability to reproduce a design freely is at once a weakness and a virtue – a weakness which allowed the influential John Ruskin's jibe that its manufacture lacks craftsmanship, and a virtue because decorative material can be made at a fraction of the cost of individually wrought pieces. However, artistry and craftsmanship are involved in the designing and carving of the patterns, and skill is necessary to produce good smooth castings. The process of carving the patterns and casting monuments and fountains requires great skill.

Thin castings may be shattered by a laterally-directed sharp blow, but columns are capable of bearing great superimposed weight. Because of its compressive strength cast iron allowed a revolution in construction of buildings. It made possible vast iron-framed factories, warehouses and department stores (preparing the way for the steel skeleton frame, and hence for the skyscraper), and allowed railway stations to be covered by great luminous glass roofs. Complete decorative façades were erected for commercial buildings (mainly in the United States), and prefabrication of rather primitive dwellings and other buildings, including churches, became a thriving export trade.

To obtain iron suitable for working by smiths, as opposed to iron for casting, a high degree of purification of the pig-iron by reheating and 'puddling' is necessary to remove impurities, so producing iron which is, on an average, 99·855 per cent pure. It contains less carbon than cast iron, and this confers different physical properties. It is malleable when hot, and may be bent, twisted or hammered into desired shapes by smiths. At certain temperatures individual pieces may be hammered into one whole, or welded by locally applied heat. Individual cold pieces may be fixed together by rivets, bolts or bands known as ferrules. Castings may be made to imitate wrought iron, e.g. by incorporating raised bands: these serve no purpose and are really a betrayal of the intrinsic worth of cast iron.

Design

Many of the motifs of wrought iron were incorporated into patterns for moulding. Their range is illustrated in *A New Booke of Drawings*, published in 1693 by Jean Tijou, the great French smith who worked in England for Sir Christopher Wren: C- and S-scrolls, *rinceau* forms, stylized acanthus leaves, masks, grotesques, animal motifs, grapevines, floral motifs, wheatsheaves, lyres, harps, vases of flowers, personal initials, fleurs-de-lis, crowns and much else. In Paris, where nineteenth-century architecture and its ironwork were often based on eighteenth-century styles, manufacturers of cast iron even went so far as to cast leaves, flowers, and so on separately and attach them to a plainer background, echoing the effect of *repoussé* details in wrought iron. But on the whole cast iron developed heavier, more sculptural forms which were suited to its nature and for the most part could not have been made in wrought iron.

The designs of ornamental castings vary from city to city. In London's late eighteenth- and early nineteenth-century neighbourhoods simple geometrical patterns and Neo-classical motifs predominate. In mid and late nineteenth-century Paris balconies gave scope for symmetrical sweeping volutes, C- and S-scrolls. In Boston the anthemion motif is ubiquitous. In New Orleans it is the exquisite botanical patterns, added to houses from the 1850s onwards, that remain in the visitor's mind. In Australia, where most of the ironwork also dates from the second half of the nineteenth century, the patterns are many and eclectic, and balustrades often consist of series of wide panels, repeating a single self-contained design. At the time of colonial expansion the mother countries supplied castings and inspired the use of national symbols. Designs incorporating the Tudor rose, Scotch thistle, Irish shamrock and Welsh leek in ever-varying combinations throughout the British Empire provide the outstanding example.

Exports to the colonies account for such things as the presence in Bermuda and at Adelaide in Australia of bandstands made in Glasgow, and for the same balcony balustrade appearing in Britain and in Australia. But exports without colonial ties also existed: we have found ironwork in Utrecht that is illustrated in a Parisian catalogue, and in Beirut a balcony pattern advertised in Australia and a stair railing that appears to be made up of balcony balusters from Glasgow.

The design of ironwork also varies with its use. Lisbon, for instance, has many small individual balconies; in New Orleans and some other southern American cities, in Cape Town, and in Australian cities the ironwork expands to cover the front of the house, providing it with verandas, balconies, or covered walks shading the footpath and calling not only for balustrades but for columns, friezes, brackets, fringes, and, in the case of designs with doubled columns, special small patterns for the spandrels between them. In Leningrad the main display of ironwork is in the innumerable bridges that cross the canals and rivers.

Designers of cast iron have derived their patterns from the remote and the not-so-distant past, and from cultures far removed from their own. The earliest form of ornament ever was probably an imitation of basketwork woven from reeds, engraved or even impressed on primitive wet clay vessels. An imitation of woven basketwork is still used on some castings, and it forms the only ornamentation of a very deep solid frieze of a colonnade on the Melbourne Club. From Greek and Roman art, designers took particular forms of column, capital and arch, frieze and entablature, and also a rich repertory of decorative pattern – plant forms such as the anthemion, palmette and acanthus, swirling foliage scrolls, plain geometrical forms like the Greek key or meander, and much else. Illustrations in *The Smith and Founder's Director*, published by the English architect and antiquary L. N. Cottingham in 1824, illustrate examples of ancient ornament suitable for conversion into ironwork patterns.

Cottingham also illustrates details from the Middle Ages including floral bosses, beautiful naturalistic foliage capitals, cresting and finials. The caster could also use Gothic tracery for fences, staircase railings and balustrades. From the Renaissance the nineteenth-century designer took symmetrical compositions with realistic and legendary birds, animals and even grotesques, interlace patterns and strapwork. Baroque features add interest and excitement, but are rare.

'Exotic' foreign styles became fashionable in the eighteenth and nineteenth centuries. Chinese design influenced graphic arts and furniture; archaeology led to an interest in ancient Egypt; and the Moorish style of Granada seemed suitable for a large cast-iron pavilion to represent Spain in the Paris Exhibition of 1889 (now in Mexico City). The Aesthetic Movement began in London in the 1860s under the impetus of Japanese art; by the 1880s radiant suns and sunflowers were ubiquitous, and appear not infrequently in Australian ironwork.

Finally, at the end of the nineteenth century, eighteenth-century styles were sometimes deliberately revived: ironwork may show medallions derived from the work of the Adam brothers, or garlands hanging from plain geometrical scrolls in the manner of French wrought iron of the age of Louis XVI.

When closely examining the design of cast iron balusters and friezes, it is interesting to apply some of the 'General Principles in the Arrangement of Form in Architecture and the Decorative Arts' put forward by Owen Jones, the English architect and theorist of design, in *The Grammar of Ornament*, published in 1856:

(3) As Architecture, so all works of the Decorative Arts, should possess fitness, proportion, harmony, the result of all of which is repose.

(4) True beauty results from that repose which the mind feels when the eye, the intellect, and the affections, are satisfied from the absence of any want.

(5) Construction should be decorated. Decoration should never be purposely constructed.
That which is beautiful is true; that which is true must be beautiful.

(6) Beauty of form is produced by lines growing out one from the other in gradual undulations: there are no excrescences; nothing could be removed and leave the design equally good or better.

(7) The general forms being first cared for, these should be subdivided and ornamented by general lines; the interstices may then be filled in with ornament, which may again be subdivided and enriched for closer inspection.

(8) All ornament should be based upon a geometrical construction.

(9) As in every perfect work of architecture a true proportion will be found to reign between all members which compose it . . .

(10) Harmony of forms consists in the proper balancing, and contrast of, the straight, the inclined and the curved.

(11) In surface decoration all lines should flow out of a parent stem. Every ornament, however distant, should be traced to its branch and root. *Oriental practice.*

(12) All junctions of curved lines with curved or of curved lines with straight should be tangential to each other. *Natural law. Oriental practice in accordance with it.*

(13) Flowers or other natural objects should not be used as ornament, but conventional representations founded upon them sufficiently suggestive to convey the intended image to the mind, without destroying the unity of object they are employed to decorate. Universally obeyed in the best periods of art, equally violated when art declines.

2 The British Isles

The earliest of all English architectural cast ironwork, as far as is known, is the railing of baluster form which was made in 1714 to surround St Paul's Cathedral in London. It was manufactured in the Sussex Weald – an ancient ironmaking area before the Industrial Revolution – by Richard Jones, and was probably designed by Thomas Robinson, who had worked under Sir Christopher Wren and Tijou. The complete fence, which weighed just over 207 tons, cost £11,608 6s. 6d., patterns, cartage and erection costing a further £125 18s. Fortunately much of the fence still remains. Wren disapproved of the use of a cast iron railing, and indeed his determination to have a wrought iron fence was one element in the quarrel that led to his dismissal. In this way the conflict between the two materials began, and it was hotly carried on for many years. The use of wrought iron for balconies goes back about a century earlier, and seems to have been introduced by Inigo Jones, who had seen examples in Venice. About 1687 Jean Tijou brought to England the French mode of working iron, and his publication *A New Booke of Drawings* (1693) tended to disseminate his Baroque style. Perhaps it was too flamboyant for the English, for his influence in London waned rather quickly, although persisting longer in the provinces.

Early domestic balustrades of wrought iron were usually simple in design, requiring minimal labour in manufacture, and were therefore relatively inexpensive. Primarily they served a protective function, and design was, in effect, an epiphenomenon. Yet these designs, being simple, admirably suited the material, often conferring an austere elegance. The early designs of cast iron tended to imitate simple wrought iron patterns. As more and more iron was required attempts were made to provide variety, and cast ironwork became more elaborate. By the end of the eighteenth century cast iron had almost replaced wrought iron on the balconies which were becoming such a feature of the terrace houses of London.

A little needs to be said of the domestic architecture of the cast iron era, which consists predominantly of individual houses united into terraces. Sir John Summerson in *Georgian London* points out that the London Building Act of 1774 enforced a structural code whereby buildings were categorized into four 'rates', each with specific limits of value and floor area, providing accommodation for all sections of the urban population. The difference between the rates was more pronounced internally than in the façades. This led to monotony, but it ensured order and dignity. The Act also limited ornament: wood ornament was banished, or kept to a minimum, when it was needed for shop fronts, window frames and door-cases. Hence detail was restrained, and in keeping with the spirit of the terrace.

Throughout the eighteenth and nineteenth centuries the estates of wealthy owners were subdivided into streets and squares for building. Brick was the usual material in London and Dublin, stone being too costly except for special purposes, but Edinburgh is a town of stone terraces. After about 1770 stucco might be used to improve the appearance of brick, either to decorate it (as the Adam brothers did in the Adelphi, their grand speculative housing scheme in London begun in 1768) or to disguise it, by simulating, with horizontal and vertical grooving, the more expensive stone. From the Regency period onwards, stucco became a fashionable surfacing material for entire buildings, epitomized by Nash's splendid terraces around Regent's Park in London and the architecture of spa or seaside towns like Cheltenham and Brighton.

Plates 48, 107
Plate 97

Plates, 35, 36

Plate 40
Plates 73, 77–81

The *Works in Architecture* of Robert and James Adam, published in 1773 and 1779, display their style, based on a new and delicate interpretation of ancient Greek and Roman architecture, which had far-reaching effects on British and North American architecture. They used cast iron extensively, synthesizing it with their building and décor, and the *Works* contain a few examples of ornamental architectural ironwork. They were closely connected with the Carron Ironworks in Scotland (see p. 22) – their elder brother John had become a partner in 1764 – and it is probable that their ideas permeated the ornamental side of that foundry's work. They designed balcony panels, usually of a classical design, railings, lamp holders and fanlights incorporating urns, swags, anthemion (stylized honey-suckle), and round or oval paterae, reminiscent of their delicate interior decoration. On the *Lancet* offices in Adelphi a bold anthemion pattern appears in the iron window guards and in the stucco of the pilasters. Robert Adam (1728–92) is usually regarded as having been the chief designer.

Plate 86

Plates 35, 36

It was the need for cheap ironwork for the vast new housing schemes which gave cast iron its economic, if not its aesthetic, victory over wrought iron. Repetitive items of innumerable patterns could be accurately reproduced in any required number at a small fraction of the cost of wrought iron.

The form of building determined the arrangement of the ironwork. The terrace houses were provided with basement areas bridged to give access to the main doorway. Iron palisades prevented the passer-by from falling into the area and provided a more attractive appearance than a solid fence or wall, and moreover let light through to basement windows. However the characteristic form of iron-work is the first floor unroofed balcony. It gave access to open air and sunlight, was a useful aid to window cleaning, and when it ran along a row it served as a means of escape in case of fire. The windows of upper floors did not extend down to floor level, and were, at the most, provided with window guards.

Plates 93, 107

Plates 41–47

In the Regency era the decorative advantages of a roofed balcony were perceived. The roof, of light appearance, was supported by thin round or openwork iron columns. The latter often appear so delicate that the word filigree comes to mind as an appropriate description. However, the roof tended to reduce light in the front rooms. Probably for this reason the balconies were usually narrow and tall; but even so the roof covering has often been removed, especially in Dublin.

Plates 48, 49, 74

Plates 107, 110

Plate 116

Plates 62, 63, 82

The nineteenth century also brought a vast expansion of the uses of cast iron, including lamp-posts for the newly developed coal gas, and even gas-works meters, which were sometimes given the dignified form of temples in cast iron. Railway stations and covered markets provided a vast field for opportunity and invention. It had, none the less, to contend with the prejudice of the connoisseurs. In *The Seven Lamps of Architecture* (1849) John Ruskin pontificated against the use of cast iron, considering any nation uncivilized which would use 'these vulgar and cheap substitutes for real decoration'.

Figure 1   Four alternative designs for fanlights, from Ornamental Iron Work, *published* c. *1975 by I. and J. Taylor in their 'Architectural Library'. They produced books for architects and builders that range from designs for chimney-pieces to a costing guide and a pocket edition of the Building Act of 1774.*

Pattern books and catalogues

Throughout the eighteenth century, lavishly illustrated books published the designs of leading architects and provided patterns for their imitators. In 1723–24 an English translation of Sebastien Le Clerc's *A Treatise of Architecture with Remarks and Observations* appeared. He illustrates some grilles and balconies, and observes that 'Balconies of Iron will do much better than those of stone, as being lighter and less subject to Decay: If they be gilt, they will be exceedingly magnificent, and a proper Ornament for a Palace.'

In 1726 James Gibbs enclosed his London church of St Martin-in-the-Fields with a cast railing that consists of weighty balusters alternating with slender rods. In 1728 he produced *A Book of Architecture*, and in it he showed a series of superlative gates and railings of restrained design, two designs for a cast iron railing for a great stair, and a wrought iron gate and overthrow.

A Complete Body of Architecture by Isaac Ware, published in 1756, was the first architectural treatise to make a positive statement about cast iron:

> Cast iron is very serviceable to the builder and a vast expense is saved in many cases by using it; in rails and balusters it makes a rich and massy appearance when it has cost very little and when wrought iron, much less substantial, would cost a vast sum.

The *Works in Architecture* of the Adam brothers has already been noted. It was among the most influential architectural books of the century. Among its design progeny was a delightful but fragile booklet of twenty-one plates published by I. and J. Taylor without introduction or text. The cover paper with its beautiful

Figure 1

copperplate lettering is undated; John Harris suggests *c.* 1795. It reads: *Ornamental Iron Work, or Designs in the Present Taste, for Fan-Lights, Stair-case railing, Window-guard-irons, Lamp-irons, Palisades, & Gates. With a Scheme for adjusting Designs with facility and accuracy to any slope.* The drawings are delicate and it is difficult to tell whether wrought or cast iron was intended. It was left to the artisan to copy as he wished. Coming at a time when the use of cast iron was beginning to expand enormously, it is safe to assume that I. and J. Taylor had in mind cast iron with, in some items, supporting bars of wrought iron.

L. N. COTTINGHAM

In 1823 Lewis Nockalls Cottingham published *The Ornamental Metal Workers' Director*, the first edition of a pattern book that was to influence design from North America to Australia. Cottingham (1787–1847) was an architect and antiquary, who published a number of books on medieval architecture and was involved in many restorations, including those of Rochester and Hereford Cathedrals. He built his house in Waterloo Bridge Road to contain his private collection of medieval woodcarvings and plaster casts of classical capitals and sculptural ornamentation. A catalogue was published in 1850, and the collection became the nucleus first of the Royal Architectural Museum and then of the Victoria and Albert Museum's collection.

The preface to *The Ornamental Metal Workers' Director* explains the book's origin and aims:

THE extensive application of metal, in securing, decorating, and furnishing every class of building, from the superb palace of the monarch to the social villa of the retired citizen, renders any apology for introducing a Work of this description unnecessary. The great improvement that has taken place in our Brass and Iron Foundries within these last twenty years, has elevated this branch of English manufacture far above that of any other country, and raised the articles which were formerly considered as merely gross and ponderous, into the scale of ornamental embellishment, in which utility and security are united with the lightness and elegance of classical design. The fidelity and correctness with which the Smiths and Ornamental Metal-workers execute their orders, must make a work, which is calculated to improve their taste, and excite emulation in getting up their patterns, generally useful and beneficial; and the decided favour that has ever been shown by gentlemen of fortune and liberal minds, to the ingenious artisan and aspiring tradesman, who are capable of combining utility and elegance in the various articles for domestic purposes, has been a sufficient stimulus to the Author to use every means in his power to introduce such a collection of Designs and Patterns as may be a guide to them in forming correct and tasteful compositions, the only way to insure a preference for the British manufacture in every class, and prevent the inundation of foreign goods, which have long obstructed the rising fame of our artists in the higher departments of this art.

Many of the subjects introduced in this Work have been executed from the designs of the most eminent artists; and those composed by the Author are from the best specimens of antique ornament, consisting of Entrance Gates to public buildings, parks, gardens, &c. Verandas, Fences: Balcony, Area, and

Figure 2   Detail of a plate from Cottingham's The Smith and Founder's Director, *1824, showing 'Gothic Capitals, Rosettes, enriched Battlements, Friezes . . . from Drawings and Casts in the Author's Possession'.*

Window Guards; Balustrades and Newels for staircases and galleries; Fanlights, Lamps and Brackets for entrance doors; Street Lamps; grand Stands for gas-lights; Tripods, Candelabra, Candlesticks, Chandeliers; Vases and Pedestals; Hot-air Stoves for churches, chapels, and public offices; elegant Stoves and Fenders for drawing rooms, &c. &c. serviceable for ladies and gentlemen to select from, and equally so to the furnishing Ironmonger. To remove in some measure the severe and painful regret that has long been felt by ingenious workmen, for the want of a collection of good ornaments to select from, at a price within the compass of their limited means, the Author has given several hundred specimens of the choicest productions of the Grecian, Etruscan, Roman and Gothic schools of art; from accurate drawings and casts in his possession, which he flatters himself will tend to facilitate the operations of the professional artist, and afford ample matter for the mechanic to study from, to whom it will be excellent practice to draw the smaller ornaments three or four times the size given in this work.

L. N. C.

66, *Great Queen Street, Lincoln's Inn Fields*
October 10th, 1823.

Plates 2–6, 8
Figure 2
Plates 7, 9

The *Ornamental Metal Workers' Director* contained sixty plates. In 1824 Cottingham published a second edition of this work, called *The Smith and Founder's Director*, to which twenty-two plates were added. We also have in our possession a number of line and wash drawings by Cottingham for balusters, staircases, verandas and balconies. The colours shown in the wash drawings indicate that ironwork was often painted in shades of yellow, green and brown.

Cottingham's genius lay in the recognition that such an apparently graceless material as iron could be transformed by the founder's hands into both simple and complex patterns and forms. He combined a great understanding of ferrous technology with the art of the carver of patterns and the craftsmanship of the technician. Columns and capitals of iron could not be distinguished by sight alone from the originals carved out of stone. He helped to popularize forms of architectural ornament which, because cheap, were to transform the face of architecture in the remainder of the nineteenth century.

HENRY SHAW

Henry Shaw's *Examples of Ornamental Metal Work*, published in London in 1836, is a collection of beautifully drawn examples, designed by Shaw himself and by the architects Sir Robert Smirke (designer of the British Museum), Bridgens, James Savage, I. Goldicutt and Charles Inwood, and executed by T. W. and L. Cubitt, Bramah and Son and others. Included in the fifty plates are locks, escutcheons, door handles, Parisian door knockers and two doors in the Rue de Richelieu, Paris. The volume is invaluable in documenting the designers, builders, and location of ironwork. The baluster shown as no. 2 in plate 13, for instance, was in the London house of Thomas Hope, the prominent art collector, designer and champion of the Greek Revival and the Picturesque, and author of *Household Furniture and Interior Decoration* (1807). Curiously, a stair baluster shown in Cottingham appears in reverse as a component of a railing in Shaw's book. Shaw (1800–1873) was himself noted as an architectural draughtsman, engraver, illuminator and antiquary.

Plates 10–13

If Cottingham and Shaw represent the repertory of the first half of the century, that of the second is contained in the catalogues of the Coalbrookdale Company of Shropshire and of a number of Scottish firms. Many important foundries produced castings in Scotland: four in Glasgow and one in Edinburgh are especially notable. All provided castings for a wider area than their own cities.

Plates 14–32

THE COALBROOKDALE COMPANY

The foundry which took its name from a small Shropshire dale is probably the world's most famous foundry, for it is associated, through its ironmasters Abraham Darby I and II, with inventions which made casting possible on a commercial scale (see p. 11).

Figure 3   Two balcony railings, from the Coalbrookdale Company's Catalogue of Castings and Works in Metal, *1875. Castings recalling the alternate balusters in the design on the left will be seen in Sydney (pl. 379).*

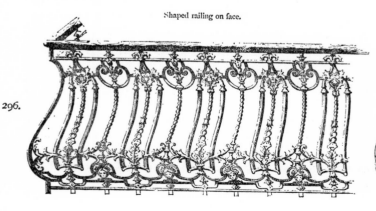

296.

199.

Plates 14–16
Figure 3

Plates 10–13

The magnificent catalogue in our possession, dated 1875, is Section V of a twelve-section series illustrating the wares of the foundry. It has 572 pages (some blank), is 28·4 cm high and 33·3 cm wide (11 3/16 × 13 3/16 inches), and weighs about 4½ kg, over 10 lb. Some fine designs appear, but as occurs with other ornamental work, satiety provokes a desire for ever greater variety, which as time passes fails to maintain a good standard. Hence a certain coarseness results, which contrasts with the early perfection exemplified by the more delicate work of Henry Shaw.

THE CARRON COMPANY

In 1759 Dr John Roebuck, Samuel Garbett and William Cadell, respectively Birmingham medical man, businessman and ironmaster, set up an ironworks on the banks of the River Carron, near Falkirk, a site chosen because of its proximity to sources of ironstone, limestone and coal, and the availability of transport. Throughout they specialized in ordnance, and cast domestic stoves and grates for which they are famous to this day. In the early years James Watt, with the assistance of Dr Roebuck, used the Carron foundry in his attempts to make a successful steam engine. By 1777 the principal product and export of the foundry was ordnance, and for the safe conduct of their cannon during the American War of Independence the company fitted out well-armed ships, which became the basis of a line between Scotland and London, carrying passengers and other merchandise. As early as 1764 John Adam was a partner in the firm, and his brothers therefore used it (as we have seen, p. 17) for the production of their masterpieces of delicate cast iron ornamentation. Perhaps of even more importance to the firm was William Haworth, one of three generations of carvers of great artistry, who commenced work at the foundry in 1781.

The introductions to catalogues, with their uniformly stilted commercial phraseology, make appealing reading. In 1891 the Carron catalogue proudly announced:

> CARRON COMPANY beg to intimate that they have been engaged for several years past making extensive alterations and improvements on their Works and Plant, which have had the effect of increasing their powers of production so as to meet the many demands made upon them, and which hitherto they have been unable to supply.
>
> The Works have been entirely reconstructed and reorganized, and the Manufacturing Departments refitted with the most approved Machinery and Appliances, calculated to effect economy in production and to maintain the high quality which CARRON COMPANY'S Goods are admitted to possess. The Foundries are in direct communication with the entire railway system of the United Kingdom, and are in close proximity to the ports of Grangemouth and Bo'ness.
>
> CARRON COMPANY smelt a high-class Pig Iron from the native ores of Scotland, with a suitable admixture of Hematite, and select therefrom a class especially adapted for their Castings. For its mechanical properties this Iron is unsurpassed by any other Scotch Brand, and with proper treatment produces the very best Castings.
>
> Extensive Warehouses are established at the Works and at London, where large Stocks are always maintained.

CARRON COMPANY have not hitherto approached any of the British Colonies: this they now do, and an entirely new and descriptive Catalogue of Goods suitable for the Colonial Markets is herewith issued.

From the reputation that has attended their business dealings for the past 132 years, the CARRON Brand and Trade Mark is now well known, and they approach their Colonial friends with the greatest confidence.

Special attention will be paid to the Packing of Goods for Export.

> CARRON, STIRLINGSHIRE, N.B.,
> *March, 1891.*

The catalogue shows a wide range of well-designed castings ranging from stoves to garden furniture. Unfortunately, possibly because of lack of interest in balustrades in 1891, very little decorative cast iron is included. A few brackets are illustrated, and are termed shelf brackets. Three railings and gates are shown. A complete gate, 3 feet in width, with locking and hanging standards, fitted with lock and key, was priced at 65s. 3d. a set.

MCDOWALL, STEVEN & CO., MILTON IRON WORKS, GLASGOW
The Milton Iron Works were established in 1834, and their catalogue, *Architectural & General Iron Castings*, ran to more than twenty editions.

Plate 30

WALTER MACFARLANE & CO., SARACEN FOUNDRY, GLASGOW
We have in our possession several publications of the Saracen Foundry (see p. 325), which are rich in interest. The astonishing façade of the foundry at Possilpark is shown in plate 18. The preface to the sixth edition of the catalogue (1882–83) states:

Plates 18–27, 468, 478
Figures 4, 5

> The legitimate development and application of Metal Work have been carefully studied and followed as a profession by Mr. Macfarlane for the last fifty years, the first six being devoted to Gold and Silver Work, the next fourteen to Hammered Iron, and the last thirty to Cast Iron in its various branches, including the decorative treatment of its surface, by colour, gilding, &c. Metals, like men, develop their power only through successive stages, and we must not lose sight of the fact that Cast Iron as applied to the decorative arts is still in its infancy, dating back only a very limited period, but, that it has a great future before it, we think the following pages amply testify. There is perhaps no other branch of the industrial arts in this country that has made such progress within the last thirty years, and as its pioneers we feel a natural pride in the success of our efforts, our Architectural, Sanitary, and General Castings having become prominent objects, not only in this country, but over the world, notable for their fresh ironlike features, sharp, clean, and full of character, neither care nor expense having been spared in the perfecting of our Designs and Patterns, our ambition being to produce the best quality of work at a moderate price.

Several editions of the catalogue show that Macfarlane's registered a number of designs, which as we shall see was necessary to prevent piracy. Macfarlane's also

Plate 19

Figure 4 The trademark of Walter Macfarlane & Co., Saracen Foundry, Glasgow.
Figure 5 A drinking fountain, registered by Macfarlane's in 1860, as shown in their Examples Book *(1876). The design was copied in Australia, with a simpler water basin, and will be seen in Melbourne (pl. 414). A larger version also existed (pls. 26 and 462).*

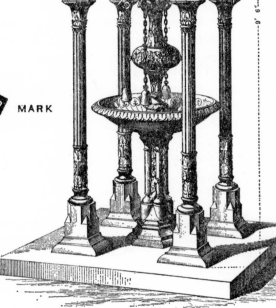

ON EVERY CASTING.

TRADE · WALTER MAC FARLANE & Cº · GLASGOW · SARACEN FOUNDRY · MARK

Figure 4

Plates 468, 478
Plates 431–436, 447, 448, 462

had a distinctive trademark, said to appear on every casting. (But a trademark did not prevent copying of the design: other firms were only prohibited from using the trademark itself on their own castings.) They exported widely, and references to the castings will be found in the sections on Australia and India. For India they produced specially designed complete buildings in 'Indian' style; in Australia we shall find a mixture of imports bearing Macfarlane's trademark and of copies of Macfarlane designs – whether produced under licence or pirated is uncertain.

The *Examples Book of Macfarlane's Castings* illustrates many extremely interesting iron buildings. An inscription indicates that it was printed before 1874, but some registration marks included give the date 1875.

GEORGE SMITH & CO., SUN FOUNDRY, GLASGOW

Plates 28, 29

Plates 87, 96, 101, 104–106, 493, 494

George Smith & Co. produced a superb *Catalogue of Architectural and Ornamental Castings*, which includes examples of executed works as well as designs. Unfortunately, like so many catalogues, it is undated. A number of balusters associated with the Sun Foundry will be seen later.

WATSON, GOW & CO., ETNA FOUNDRY, GLASGOW

Plates 31, 32

Watson, Gow & Co., of Lily Bank Road, produced a catalogue with fine lithographed illustrations, including a large number of narrow balusters. Of particular interest is a composite illustration showing a veranda and balcony, for one of the patterns shown there has parallels in Australia, at Sydney and in Tasmania.

Plate 31
Plate 32
Plates 362, 458

CHARLES D. YOUNG & CO., EDINBURGH

A Short Treatise on the System of Wire Fencing, Gates, Etc., and an *Illustrated and Descriptive Catalogue of Ornamental Cast and Wrought Iron and Wire Work* were published by Young's in 1850. Still more fascinating is their compilation, *Illustrations of Iron Structures, for Home and Abroad* (see pp. 62–63, 65), in which the magnificent prefabricated Corio Villa, erected at Geelong in Australia, appears, together with other portable buildings.

Plates 344–350
Figure 11

Registration marks

As we have seen, trademarks were not sufficient to prevent copying of designs. As a safeguard, registration was instituted, and between 1842 and 1883 iron fabrications were registered at the Patents Office in the same manner as objects in wood, glass and ceramics.

Plates 17, 19

The registration mark took the form of a lozenge with a circle at the top. In the circle, roman numerals I to IV indicated the 'class' or material of the object. Iron is in class I. Up to 1868 the letter below the class number gave the year of manufacture. The day of the month is recorded in the right-hand corner, while the month is indicated in the left-hand corner. The figure at the bottom indicates the manufacturer, who may also be recorded elsewhere on the casting. A notable example is A. Kenrick, whose name is impressed into all his castings, such as a large range of door knockers.

From 1868 to 1883 the figure below the class number indicates the day of the month of manufacture, while the letter at the bottom indicates the month and the letter in the right-hand corner gives the year. The figure opposite it on the left may be the manufacturer's identification or a parcel number.

The code for year and month, which remained constant, is as follows:

Year letters:

1842	X	1856	L	1870	C
1843	H	1857	K	1871	A
1844	C	1858	B	1872	I
1845	A	1859	M	1873	F
1846	I	1860	Z	1874	U
1847	F	1861	R	1875	S
1848	U	1862	O	1876	V
1849	S	1863	G	1877	P
1850	V	1864	N	1878	D
1851	P	1865	W	1879	Y
1852	D	1866	Q	1880	J
1853	Y	1867	T	1881	E
1854	J	1868	X	1882	L
1855	E	1869	H	1883	K

Month letters:

January	C	May	E	September	D
February	G	June	M	October	B
March	W	July	I	November	K
April	H	August	R	December	A

Thus the mark on the casting shown at the bottom in plate 17 indicates that it was registered on 12 April 1853. The mark appears frequently in Scottish catalogues: that in plate 19 gives a date of 3 June 1867.

London

Plates 35, 36

Early eighteenth-century London had been a city of relatively small-scale development in the form of two- and three-storey terraces and a few squares. As we have seen, in 1768 the Adam brothers began their riverside complex of elegant terrace houses, the Adelphi. A number of estates were built up, such as the Duke of Bedford's land in Bloomsbury, but the next bold architectural venture was that of John Nash (1752–1835), who, from 1812 to *c.* 1830, united grand terrace houses and commercial buildings into breathtaking white façades in his magnificently conceived town-planning schemes which provided one of London's chief glories.

Plates 37–40

He followed classical precedents, but aimed at the picturesque. His essay in planning extended from the East and West Park Villages in the north around and through Regent's Park, along Park Square and around Park Crescent to fuse into the already developed Portland Place, then on to unify Regent Street, finally ending at St James's Park. Fortunately a great deal of his architecture towards the north has remained. Whether he designed the ironwork for his buildings (some of which appears in Cottingham), or used commercially available castings, will probably never be known.

The subdivision of the great estates to house the expanding population of London contributed greatly to the style of the city, which has persisted to the present day. Fortunately skilled architects and builders were often employed to produce the terraces of houses of varying 'rates' (see p. 16): drabness of the lower rates and uniformity of all rates may be challenged, but when well kept the

Plates 41–43

formal exteriors, with their sparse cast iron ornamentation, contribute to a restful street scene.

The uniformity of the pattern of cast iron over large areas of one estate is an interesting feature. Large orders of the same pattern would be placed to obtain it more cheaply, to give uniformity and possibly sometimes to save bother. However, when construction was done in stages, different patterns would appear in the same estate. This is clearly seen in the Thurloe Estate, South Kensington, which

Plates 52–54

has been studied in great detail by Dorothy Stroud (*The Thurloe Estate*, 1959). The estate has undergone many changes, chiefly in the hands of John Alexander, who received part of it by inheritance and considerably enlarged the holdings. George Basevi (1794–1845) contributed effectively to its architecture. A first cousin of Benjamin Disraeli, he worked in the office of Sir John Soane from 1810 to 1816, and toured Greece and Italy subsequently. Hence he was well grounded in the classical tradition.

The same ironwork design may appear on different estates: a pattern found on the Thurloe Estate, for instance, recurs on the New River Estate, far to the north-east in Islington. Myddleton Square on the New River Estate was designed by William Mylne in 1827, and has recently been restored to its earlier elegance.

Throughout this book ornamental cast iron plays a subservient role to architecture. Rarely does it rise to the status of a great independent work. It is all the more tragic that one of the supreme creations in cast iron, which stood in the City of London until 1962, was wantonly destroyed by a Corporation ignorant of its value and unable to appreciate its quality. The iron rotunda of the Coal Exchange, in Lower Thames Street, was built in 1846–49 by the City Corporation's architect, J. B. Bunning. He united external masonry and an internal iron cage rising to a glazed iron-ribbed dome. Around the vast central area series of cast iron galleries fronted offices. The ubiquitous ironwork of the galleries was of rope design. Paintings around the base of the dome represented primordial vegetation which eventually became coal, and other paintings showed various phases of coal mining.

Plates 64, 65

The building was doomed in 1961, to allow road widening. The usual propaganda techniques were followed: the building was stigmatized by the Chairman of the Streets Committee as 'this dingy, brown-painted miserable place'; he had seen better ironwork in public houses, he said: the Exchange would not have been accepted by his Committee as a public lavatory. It was even suggested that as a monument to Britain's shameful coal-mining industry the Exchange ought to be demolished! Thus one of the early monuments of iron and glass technology was destroyed. Fourteen years later, the road is still unwidened and the site remains vacant.

It could have provided a unique display area for a museum of cast iron fabrications. An attempt to bring the building to Melbourne, Australia, as part of the projected Cultural Centre failed because of derogatory statements in the press made by ignoramuses in influential positions, and lack of time to raise the necessary finance. What a unique period piece of cast iron construction was lost to posterity!

Brighton

Brighton, on the Sussex coast, developed as a seaside resort in the eighteenth century. The town was given a strong impetus by John Nash's imaginative effort of reconstruction for the Prince Regent, which produced the 'Hindoo' Royal Pavilion (1815–22), while the association with royalty made the town fashionable. In the Pavilion is to be found one of the most delicate of all essays in cast iron – a staircase in which iron is made to look as light as bamboo.

Plates 66–73

Plate 70

The Indian openwork screens of the Pavilion were taken over and recreated in cast iron by the designer of Madeira Drive, a long sheltered arcade by the sea, below Marine Parade, which was built in 1888–95. At the western end of Madeira Drive the Palace Pier of 1898–99 extends out into the sea, and beyond it lies the West Pier, begun in 1865, given more elaborate buildings later in the century, and now under very serious threat.

Plates 66–69

The remainder of Brighton is largely Regency and early Victorian, with intimate streets, squares and houses, many with bow fronts and nearly all with cast iron balconies. The houses facing the sea are spacious and are now divided into desirable apartments. The ironwork usually resembles that of London, but occasionally a different pattern, perhaps designed by the architect of the building, is to be seen.

Cheltenham

Plates 74–76

The reopening of the old wells in 1738 and the visit of George III in 1788 established the popularity of this Gloucestershire town as a fashionable spa. It developed rapidly after the turn of the century as a place of retirement, especially for people who had spent most of their life in India. Two famous architects, Decimus Burton and J. B. Papworth, played an important part in its construction. Hence it comes about that this town was designed and built up during the late Georgian period; design was then becoming more elaborate and more decorated, and acquiring those characteristics which are named Regency. The ironwork of Cheltenham is curvaceous and delicate, sometimes excessively so. Wrought iron was still used in this period, although giving way to cast iron. The transition may be clearly seen in Cheltenham, and the use of cast iron panels affixed to wrought iron frames gives further evidence of a transition period. Our best wishes must be given to local preservation societies who struggle valiantly to preserve their heritage which, although not always appreciated by authorities at the time, is a guarantee of future fame.

Leamington Spa

Plates 77–81

Leamington Spa, in Warwickshire, has many fine Georgian and Regency buildings with cast iron ornamentation. There is a remarkable concentration in Clarendon Square, with which our photographs are largely concerned. Its spacious stuccoed houses were begun about 1825, and are notable for their ornate porches and covered balconies on the first floor.

Great Malvern

As early as the seventeenth century seven springs in Malvern's six villages were believed to have therapeutic value, and the town was fully exploited as a spa in the nineteenth century.

Plate 82

While passing in an express train from Hereford to London we noticed the remarkable capitals of Great Malvern Station. This prompted return by a slow train, which was well rewarded. The Worcester–Malvern–Hereford railway line was constructed in 1860, and shortly afterwards E. W. Elmslie designed the station and a grand Gothic hotel nearby, which offered the railway traveller an alternative to the older Foley Arms inn, up in the centre of town. The capitals of the iron columns which support the platform roofs were recently repainted, after careful tests, and restored to their original brilliant naturalistic colours.

Plate 83

Edinburgh

The use of cast iron during expansion of a city in the nineteenth century is demonstrated by the New Town of Edinburgh. The first phase, begun in 1767, was bounded on the north by Queen Street and on the south by Princes Street, looking across the wide valley to the castle and the medieval town. At the eastern end was St Andrew's Square, while Charlotte Square, designed by Robert Adam in 1791, terminated the western end. This fairly small rectangular area is bisected by George Street.

Plate 86

In 1803 a second part of the New Town was begun with Heriot Row, east of Abercromby Place. It terminated in 1820 with Great King Street and India Street, both leading towards the Royal Circus, which displays a plain classical style of architecture at its loveliest. The magnificent sweep of the true circle, with its large central garden and its cobbled roads has a breathtaking elegance. Robert Reid and William Sibbald were the architects for this area, accounting for the uniformity of appearance which produces a sense of tranquillity rather than monotony. Fanlights with cast iron glazing bars and iron balconies serve to add a pleasing diversity of detail.

Plates 87, 88, 90, 91

Plate 89

Building at the south-western end of Charlotte Square was begun in 1815 and by 1830 comprised Melville Street and Manor Place. Moray Place and neighbouring streets were built as a series of stately houses in fine terraces.

Plates 92–97

The silvery or creamy grey stone of Edinburgh has at first, especially on dull days, a sombre appearance, but one comes to appreciate its Scottish clarity and solidity and, when cleaned, its great intrinsic beauty.

Victorian ironwork in the city is chiefly represented by the imposing, if relatively plain, interior of the Royal Scottish Museum of 1861. The local foundry of Charles D. Young & Co. was an important manufacturer of prefabricated iron buildings, 'for Home and Abroad' (see pp. 25 and 62–65).

Plate 100
Plates 344–350,
Figure 11

Glasgow

Glasgow illustrates the tendency to use cast iron, then freely and cheaply available, for ornamentation as the Industrial Revolution gained momentum.

Plates 101–106

Most of the cast iron ornamentation of Glasgow is to be found in a relatively small area to the west of Charing Cross and north of Sauchiehall Street. Separated from Sauchiehall Street by a public garden is Newton Place, which fronts a stuccoed terrace with iron balconies on its centre and side pavilions and balconettes on the remainder of the first floor windows. The building was designed by the Edinburgh architect, George Smith. He used the anthemion pattern common in Edinburgh for the balconettes, and a pattern cast by George Smith's Sun Foundry of Glasgow for the long balconies. A common feature in Glasgow is the use of balustrade-like patterns for area railing, which were also cast in the city.

Plates 102–104

As previously indicated, a number of important foundries in Glasgow, including Macfarlane's Saracen Foundry and George Smith's Sun Foundry, produced an enormous amount of architectural cast iron. Glasgow played an important role in the United Kingdom in the creation of prefabricated buildings, and one of the finest of all iron buildings, worthy of comparison with New York, happily still stands in Jamaica Street: the Gardner warehouse, built in 1855–56 by the architect John Baird, Sr., and the ironfounder R. McConnell.

Plates 101, 103

Plates 107–115, 117

Dublin

Merrion Square is the quintessence of Georgian Dublin, and a study of its varied ironwork is fascinating. The square itself, in fact an elongated rectangle, was laid out in 1762 and completed by about 1790. The mode of usage of cast iron – a balcony fronting French or deep sash windows on the first floor and a basement with protective railings – is similar to that of London, but the Dublin architects achieved a considerable amount of individuality in the application of cast iron to the façades and gateposts, and balconies went on being added in the Victorian *Plates 107, 110* age. The sides of the square are different, the north side being more robust, while *Plate 114* the earlier east and south sides are redolent of the delicate work of the Adam brothers.

3 The Continent of Europe

The Soviet Union: Leningrad and Moscow

Leningrad and Moscow, and particularly the former, add much to the saga of cast iron ornamentation.

Man's manipulation of geography created, in St Petersburg, a unique setting for cast iron ornamentation, which was supplemented by artistic creativeness in the design of the ironwork. After the Russian defeat by Charles XII of Sweden, Tsar Peter the Great sought a base for future operations against Swedish-occupied Finland. In May 1703 he decided upon a site on the delta of the River Neva, which divides between many islands to reach the Gulf of Finland. On this inhospitable marshy area, with fierce drive and inhumanity, he brought to birth the city of St Petersburg, which remained the principal administrative, cultural and artistic centre of the Russian Empire for over two hundred years. The multitude of canals and the great Neva itself, with fine embankments lined by Neo-classical buildings, mostly of uniform height on a level terrain, form one of the most beautiful cities in the world. The first permanent bridge over the Neva was not built until the 1840s, but by that time many smaller bridges had been built, as the marshes were filled in and drained into sixty canals which wind through the city, reputedly crossed by some six hundred bridges. Cast iron balustrades were being erected in the eighteenth century, when cast iron ornamentation was only very sparingly used elsewhere in the world. The designs followed classical traditions, for in its formative years the city's architecture was open to foreign influences, and indeed many of the architects were foreign-born (like Cameron, who worked at Catherine the Great's palace, Tsarskoye Selo) or of foreign parentage.

Plates 118–137

Plates 118, 128

Plate 118

Plate 138

In October 1917 the Socialist revolution began in the city, then called Petrograd. Subsequently the name was changed to Leningrad, and the Socialist government removed to Moscow in 1918. The city suffered severely during World War II, but was magnificently restored, and even today it continues its process of beautification with iron castings. The dates of the bridges shown in our photographs are taken from O. Kolesova's '*With iron-tracings richly wrought . . .*' (1970).

The ironwork of Moscow differs from that of Leningrad. It is a much older city – in 1947 it celebrated its eight hundredth anniversary – hence much of it was built before the cast iron era. What eye-catching cast iron motifs there are were almost all generated by the 1917 revolution, after which pride determined

Plates 139–143

Plates 140–142

the use of symbols of an emerging culture, such as the radiant five-pointed star and the hammer and sickle. In common to both cities is the massive heaviness of the castings, and the use of ornamental motifs superimposed on plain railings.

France: Paris

It seems that cast iron balconies appeared quite early in France. The *Journal de Verdun* for January 1727 states:

> Whereas ordinary balconies have only added ornaments of wrought iron, embossed sheet iron or brass, the new cast iron balconies are made in one piece and are enriched with anything of which a wooden sculpture can be made: animal figures, festoons, flowers; and those superb balconies cost less in iron than they would cost in wood.

However, it is probable that most of the ironwork was wrought before the Revolution. The French guilds had very strict rules, the craft and membership being passed on from father to son. It was thus very difficult for an outsider to gain apprenticeship and competence. This practice did not accord with revolutionary principles: the guilds ceased to exist about 1792, and among them was the guild of smiths, so that smiths were no longer trained in the art of working iron. Further, in 1793, grilles, balconies and stair balustrades, a whole heritage of wrought iron, were collected and melted down to provide iron for other uses. They were later replaced by the more easily made castings, often using the earlier balustrades as patterns. This process of replacement was very active by 1826. The secretary of the jury of the International Exhibition of 1867 stated that the almost exclusive employment of cast iron from 1825 to 1845 meant the extinction of good smiths amongst the ironworkers. It was only towards the end of the nineteenth century that there was a revival of the art of working individual pieces of iron.

Napoleon I's urban planning projects resulted in the widespread use of a style of Romantic Classicism and the infinite repetition of the same formula, the individual abutting houses or blocks of flats being box-like with flat roofs. Mansard roofs were reintroduced later and became so characteristic of Paris that a brief description is desirable. A low-pitched upper portion is based upon steeply sloping sides which are pierced by one, two or even three tiers of dormer windows. The tall space provided good headroom, and the large windows, sometimes extending down to floor level, admitted much light. Thus the arrangement was superior to the English attic room.

Plates 147, 148

Napoleon III was also concerned with the beautification of Paris, and under his direction in the mid nineteenth century Baron Haussmann created great public buildings and magnificent boulevards, lined by blocks of flats of uniform height with mansard roofs, which set the style for the subsequent expansion of the city. The façades themselves became richer, the Romantic Classical being modified by High Renaissance and Baroque features and then by delicate Rococo curves and the restrained Neo-classicism of the Louis XVI style. Large mansions (*hôtels*

Plate 149
Plate 175

particuliers), such as may be seen at the Rond Point des Champs Elysées, show fine expensive details. Central and flanking pavilion features give variety to large public buildings.

The façades of Parisian buildings are distinctive in that most windows reach down to floor level, or at least open widely: hence balconies, balconettes and window guards were necessary at all levels. There could hardly be a better demonstration of the functional value of ironwork. The ubiquitous balconies fit well into the street patterns, unobtrusive and, as elsewhere, usually unobserved. At the present time they are little used for outdoor living, although they may be used desultorily for observation of the outside world, conversation and passing the time of day with neighbours.

Plates 149–153

Plate 144

PATTERNS

Simple patterns give interest to the façades of poorer blocks of flats, but the characteristic ironwork of the more expensive blocks, built from about 1850 onwards, is more elaborate than that of London. Many of the patterns were based upon the traditional characteristics of wrought iron, with its curves and *repoussé* work. The architecture, almost all inspired by late seventeenth- and eighteenth-century styles, called for ironwork which was itself revivalist. The firm of Barbezat & Cie. note in their beautifully produced catalogue that certain motifs are cast separately and then attached – increasing the resemblance to wrought iron. A characteristic motif of French ironwork is a fairly narrow, symmetrical panel of which the side pieces end in scrolls at top and bottom. Renaissance patterns allowed the casters to break away from such close dependence, and to make use of the sculptural nature of cast iron. Almost every element of design may be found in the ironwork, including human figures, masks, animals, birds naturalistic and mythical, fruit, flowers, swags and vases. A number of such patterns are recorded in the Barbezat catalogue.

Plates 158–165

Plate 155

Plate 159
Plates 166, 181, 182

A feature of Parisian buildings is the single or double doors giving access from the street to a paved courtyard. The doors are usually provided with heavy panels of cast iron in Neo-classical or Renaissance patterns, or, at the turn of the century, consist entirely of glass and openwork patterns imitating wrought iron.

Plate 154, Figure 6

Plates 169–173

Figure 6   Balustrade panel, from the catalogue of Barbezat & Cie. A casting of this Renaissance design, with fabulous birds and serpents, occurs in Utrecht (pl. 181).

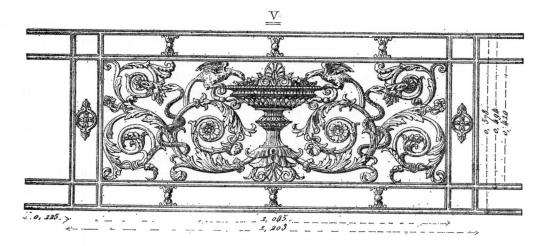

The Netherlands

Plates 177–179

Amsterdam is a city based upon a canalized river, the Amstel, that flows into an arm of the Zuider Zee. The low-lying land necessitated the formation of draining canals retained by dykes on which roads and houses were built. This physical factor, with a constant struggle against nature, determined the unique quality of Amsterdam. The need to house the large urban population in a restricted reticulated area of land determined the juxtaposition of tall and narrow abutting houses. The different types of gables, facing the canals, gave variety and produced an interesting skyline. Cast iron balconies and window guards are rare. The chief use is as balustrades for *stoeps* (steps leading up to front doors raised safely above the damp ground), waterways and bridges. Some fence posts are highly ornamental, but the majority are plain. Nevertheless, there are a multitude of slight variations, each peculiar to its own region.

Plates 180–184

Utrecht grew up as the capital of a province and the seat of a university. It has fewer canals than other cities in Holland, but the environs of the Oudegracht and the Nieuwegracht ('old canal' and 'new canal'), which run a partially parallel course near the centre of the city, are of interest.

Plate 180

A building on the Oudegracht, since 1906 the Vlaer and Kol Bank, is of special interest from the point of view of cast iron. In 1836–39 a new façade was built, with four symbolic statues high up and four caryatids at ground level. These were thought locally to be stone carvings, and our good friend and guide Dr G. W. Bruyn was astonished when a magnet adhered to them.

Portugal: Lisbon

Plates 190–196

Lisbon, capital of Portugal, on the Tagus River near its entrance into the Atlantic, was built on a series of terraces on low hills, backed by the granite mountains of Cintra.

On 1 November 1755 almost the whole of the city was destroyed by an earthquake, followed by a tidal wave and a fire which completed the destruction. Restoration began very slowly, delayed by historical events and catastrophies which affected Portugal. Amongst these were internal and external factors, including the French invasion followed by removal of the court to Rio de Janeiro, the Peninsular War, the loss of Brazil, internal revolution and dynastic troubles. It was not until 1850, well into the cast iron era, that regeneration gained momentum. Thus the history of the city explains the extent of its cast iron ornamentation.

Plate 193

The rebuilt part of the city consists largely of lofty blocks of flats or houses set in narrow streets. Most are simple in design, with flat façades and roofs of low pitch hidden behind projecting cornices or sometimes decorative parapets. Some more opulent houses have pilasters, heavy mouldings, and Italianate or Baroque features. They have a varied appearance which is increased by the colour-washing of the stucco (ochres, pinks and light greens) and the covering of

Plate 192

many façades by coloured and patterned ceramic tiles. At street intersections a curve in the façade often replaces a sharp corner. The provision of small balconies

Plate 190

for individual windows is the outstanding characteristic of the ironwork of Lisbon. The balconies, wide or narrow, jut out over the street at whatever level windows come down to floor level. Tall and short windows may be found on any floor, sometimes uniformly or symmetrically arranged, sometimes in haphazard arrangement as though their site and size depended upon the whim of the builder. Sometimes window guards are used instead of balconies. Occasionally a balcony runs across the width of the upper floor, especially in large buildings. This may have originated as a means of escape in case of fire. Roofed balconies are rare. The patterns of the balusters show no unusual features, and some have been seen in other cities.

Plate 192
Plate 193

Lisbon possesses a unique public elevator of cast iron, constructed by the famous French engineer Gustave Eiffel. Rising in a *cul-de-sac*, its two large lifts allow access, across a bridge, to a part of the city at a much higher level. The distinctive decorative ironwork was obviously part of the intrinsic design of the cage.

Plates 193–196

Greece: Athens

The ancient architecture of Greece, upon which is based so much derivative architecture throughout the world, overshadows all else in Athens. As a capital Athens revived when Greece won her independence from the Turks in 1832: the new king came from the royal family of Bavaria, and foreign architects received major commissions throughout the century. With a singular aptness, they brought back to Athens the Neo-classical forms derived from ancient Greece that were popular through Europe in the early nineteenth century. Particularly active was the Dane Theophil von Hansen, who built the Palais Dimitriou in 1842–43 (later taken over, and eventually destroyed, by the Hotel Grande-Bretagne), the Academy, National Library and a number of smaller buildings. He continued to supply designs even after he had left Athens for Vienna, and his style was carried on by his pupil, Ernst Ziller, whose house built for the archaeologist Schliemann is now the Supreme Court. The ironwork is correspondingly Greek Revival, incorporating mythical beings, swans and monsters in bold symmetrical designs.

Plate 198

Plate 197

Plate 200

Plates 197–202

Other European ironwork

In many European cities there is little cast iron ornamentation. The older cities had a great tradition of the handworking of iron, and wrought iron tended to persist throughout the nineteenth century. In areas where iron, coal and foundries were scarce, wrought iron would be preferred since less iron is used. Other regions may have no iron industry, or no interest in manufacturing or importing ironwork for more than street furniture, since the climate may discourage balconies.

Plates 203–213

The advent of illumination of streets by coal gas during the nineteenth century coincided with the cast iron era. Cast iron was an excellent material for making multitudes of lamp standards, so that importation or local manufacture made economic sense.

Plate 205

4 The United States of America

Sir Walter Raleigh is said to have sent iron ore from Roanoke Island, North Carolina, back to England for evaluation. Again in 1607 iron ore was sent to England, this time from Jamestown, Virginia. The first blast furnace in America was established at Falling Creek, Virginia, by English foundrymen, but it was wiped out by an Indian massacre before it could begin operation. It was in 1642, at what is now Hammersmith, near Lynn on the Saugus River in Massachusetts, that the first American casting was produced – the 'Saugus Pot'.

The Saugus Iron Works lasted less than forty years, failing in 1678 due partly to litigation, including nuisance suits, and partly to the lack of trees for charcoal (as in England: see below and p. 11), but it is of great interest because a few of its buildings survived, and others were reconstructed by the First Iron Works Association, Inc., formed in 1943. The establishment consisted of a giant blast furnace, finery and chafery forges, a slitting mill, the ironmaster's house, cottages for workmen, a farm and outbuildings. Trees were cut down by farmers working during the off-season, and by Scots who had been taken prisoner by Cromwell's forces at the battle of Dunbar in 1650 and sold into indentured service. Logs were converted into charcoal by slow burning in sod-covered kilns. Bog iron ore was dug from marshes and old stream beds and dense rock ore was quarried at Nahant. The latter also acted as a flux. Waterwheels provided power for the huge bellows, which blew air into the furnace with its load of alternate layers of iron ore and charcoal. When a high temperature was reached molten iron collected at the bottom, to be run off into simple moulds or branching channels (see above, p. 11). The pig-iron thus produced was transported to forges both near and far, where, after melting, it was cast into moulds of desired shape. In order to produce iron for working, the pigs were reheated to a high temperature and 'puddled' to burn off the carbon content. The iron was then beaten into 'merchant bars' by a heavy mechanical hammer. These bars could be rolled into strips or rods in the slitting mill, or be used by smiths to produce useful or decorative objects of wrought iron. At Saugus water-power was used to work the hammer and the mechanism of the slitting mill.

An interesting sidelight is the role played by iron in the establishment of the United States. In 1750 the British Parliament passed an Act prohibiting the colonies from casting iron or refining pig-iron for their own use, and restricting the building of additional furnaces and forges. Pig-iron could be legally produced only for export to England, where a shortage of charcoal had seriously curtailed production. This Act meant virtual stagnation of a country badly in need of metal fabrications. It brought forth the kind of resistance which precedes an uprising: it was openly flouted, and agents of the British Crown attempting enforcement soon lost their prestige. In *Development of the Metal Castings Industry* Bruce L. Simpson argues that these restrictions were a more fundamental cause of the American Revolution than the colonists' resentment at taxation without representation. Most foundrymen in America joined the revolutionary movement; and the importance of foundries to military success may well be imagined.

Catalogues

As in other countries, catalogues from the past add interest to the study of cast iron ornamentation. In *A Guide to American Trade Catalogues, 1744–1900*, Lawrence B. Romaine lists some twenty-six foundries producing castings such as railings, hitching posts, weathervanes, finials, lamps, garden furniture, etc. Undoubtedly the list is incomplete, but the small number of foundries listed explains the rarity of trade catalogues which have survived. Being chiefly soft-covered they were regarded as ephemeral and shared the fate of most such catalogues. A number of catalogues of iron foundries in New York are preserved in the Metropolitan Museum of Art.

Roofed verandas and balconies play an important part in the cities of the United States of America, especially in the south. Chapter IX of the catalogue of the *Iron Manufactures of the New York Wire Railing Company*, dated 1857, begins:

> *Verandahs* are portions of a country house which cannot be dispensed with, nor are they to be overlooked in preparing plans for City and Suburban residences. In one of these delightful shelters there is a sense of enjoyment to be found that can be had nowhere else. In a Country-seat especially are they needed. Through them comes the view of pleasant twilights, and the evening breezes blow sweetly among the climbing plants that cover them. Walls are hot, and fresh air is wanted under all circumstances. The Iron Verandah offers advantages which no other material can possibly furnish. Its graceful and open fabric lends ornament to the dwelling, it permits a consultation of all tasks, it impedes no current of air, and is at once substantial and elegant.

The caption to an illustration in the catalogue comments on the construction of such verandas:

Plate 218

> The figure shows how the verandah is attached to the house, when used on the second floor. The columns can be dispensed with, and brackets substituted, provided the verandah does not extend too far from the building. Columns are generally considered safer, as they support the superincumbent weight, and relieve the side of the building.

The J. L. Mott Iron Works of 84–90 Beekman Street, New York, established in 1828, produced many castings and a number of fine catalogues which, in exemplary fashion, were dated. Catalogues from other cities include those of Chase Brothers & Co. in Boston, Hayward, Bartlett & Co. and later Bartlett, Robbins

Plate 221

Plates 260, 262, 268, 270

37

Plate 290

& Co. in Baltimore (see p. 43), and the Lorio Iron Works and Hinderer's Iron Works in New Orleans (p. 47).

In looking at some of the decorative ironwork in the United States, we shall begin in New York, then travel north to Boston and south to Philadelphia, Baltimore, Georgetown, Charleston and New Orleans, finishing in California.

New York

IRON FAÇADES AND BUILDINGS

This book deals with cast iron architectural ornamentation and only incidentally with façades or buildings constructed of cast iron; but the ornamentation of some of the cast iron façades of New York justifies their admission here. Nowhere else in the world is there such a concentration of cast iron façades and complete buildings as in lower Manhattan. Fortunately the Friends of Cast-Iron Architecture have directed their energies to the discovery, documentation and preservation of such buildings, working, as elsewhere in the world, against official neglect and tardiness and vested financial interests. The future will bless them for their successes. The chairman of the organization, Margot Gayle, wrote in *Americana*:

Plates 214, 322–326

> Typically, iron fronts were used for stores, offices, warehouses, and even hotels, and were wildly popular for some thirty years, from the 1850s through the 1880s. How the nineteenth-century businessman must have liked these ornate, sometimes actually palatial-looking buildings. Many of them were designed in Renaissance style, replete with columns and cornices, balustrades and brackets, arched windows and pediments. Costly stone carvings and overblown decorations could be reproduced in cast iron at a modest price – and, when painted a light color, actually did look like stone.
>
> Yet cast iron never seems to have caught on for residential construction. From the beginning, it was associated with manufacturing and public works, as in the building of mills and factories and bridges in the late eighteenth century in England. By the mid-nineteenth century, when it took root in the United States, iron architecture already had a totally commerical connotation . . .
>
> Incredibly, New York City's lower Manhattan – where building up and tearing down has always seemed a way of life – is the greatest repository of the remaining nineteenth-century iron buildings. At least two hundred, some of them truly magnificent, are found south of 23rd Street. Among former grand department stores is the 1868 McCreery Building on Broadway at 11th Street, now undergoing transformation to a luxury apartment house. Another, Stern Brothers' 1878 big white iron front near Madison Square, is well kept by its occupant, the New York Merchandise Company . . .
>
> In SoHo (an acronym for South of Houston Street) are numerous interesting iron warehouses built after the Civil War to house the city's large wholesale textile business. Most were designed by noted architects, who were often the best of the period. Today, artists are using some of the lofts and ground-floor stores as studios and galleries, while others are occupied by small industries.

The Da Capo Press has done more than justify its purpose with its publication of *The Origins of Cast Iron Architecture in America*, reproducing *Illustrations of Iron*

Plate XCVII

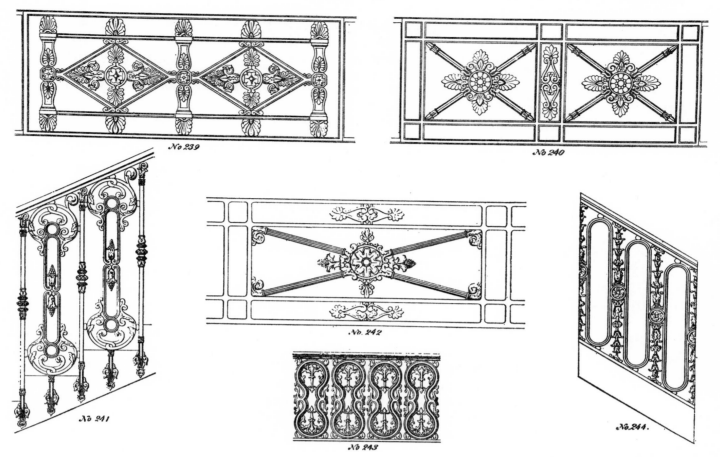

No 239

No 240

No 241

No. 242

No 243

No.244.

Lith of Sarony, Major & Knapp 449 Broadway N.Y.

ARCHITECTURAL IRON WORKS - NEW YORK

Figure 7 'Railings for balustrades and stoops', from Daniel D. Badger's Illustrations of Iron
Architecture, Made by the Architectural Iron Works of the City of New York, *1865.
The designs top and centre are still classical in derivation, and recall illustrations by Cottingham
(compare pl. 2).*

Architecture, Made by the Architectural Iron Works of the City of New York (Daniel D.
Badger, President) published in 1865, and *Cast Iron Buildings: Their Construction
and Advantages* (1856), a pamphlet putting forward the ideas of James Bogardus,
perhaps written by John W. Thomson. The brief preface to Badger's *Illustrations*
states:

> It is well known that Iron has been used in England and other European
> countries for *interior* supports in various kinds of edifices, in the form of columns,
> beams, etc.; but its introduction for the *exterior* of buildings is believed to be of
> purely *American* invention . . .
>   The first person who practically used Iron as a building material for the
> exterior was Daniel D. Badger.

However, the Bogardus pamphlet states that he was the inventor of the first
complete cast iron building in the world, an iron model being freely exhibited in

*Plates 215–217,
Figure 7*

1847, and the building erected in 1848. Bogardus was not a founder himself, but an engineer and designer, who had his designs executed by various firms.

In his introduction to the Da Capo volume Walter Knight Sturges writes:

Plate 215

> Daniel Badger's ideas were quite simple. With his team of anonymous architectural designers, modelers, and molders, he sought to reproduce at a lower cost in iron whatever could be produced in stone. If stone had hand cut ornament, iron could achieve the same result by mass production. Iron was strong and apparently fireproof. Its forms could be attenuated without risk of structural failure, and as a result, without sacrificing architectural elegance, more light could be admitted than in more conventional buildings. If the iron front grew drab from accumulations of soot and dirt, all it needed was a coat of paint to fresh–it up and make it look new.

Apparently this splendid facet of Americana was forgotten until revived by the Friends of Cast-Iron Architecture.

Plates 224–238

ORNAMENTAL IRONWORK IN NEW YORK

There is much ornamental cast iron in domestic areas of New York. It is not surprising that many architectural and decorative styles should be represented, from Neo-classical buildings with Georgian affinities to brownstone terraces built in the later nineteenth century. Originality in ironwork is displayed chiefly in the fences, newel posts and balustrades of the stoops, or raised entrances (derived from the Dutch *stoep*: see p. 34). French windows on the first floor may give access to balconettes or to balconies running across the width of the façade, and roofed

Plates 226, 233, 302

balconies with openwork columns similar to those of New Orleans are occasionally found.

The ornamental castings of New York tend to be heavy, with strong design, but are far from lacking in grace. Some patterns have the airy lightness reminiscent of the common type of New Orleans.

Boston, Massachusetts

The Pilgrim Fathers landed in Massachusetts in 1620, there forming one of the earliest English settlements, later to be supplemented by more immigrants from England. Hence architecture tended to reflect English styles, vernacular or sophisticated, modified by local conditions. Wood was the building material at hand, and the frame house covered by boarding became the American prototype. The façade was usually symmetrical and the central portal classical in inspiration. Reproduction of the English Georgian house in wood was one of America's first contributions to architecture. The later houses, built of brick or stone, still preserve the same Georgian qualities. Cast iron ornamentation came much later, in the nineteenth century, and played a considerable part in the architecture of Boston.

Almost nothing of seventeenth- and eighteenth-century Boston remains. Boston of the nineteenth century provides a fascinating architectural study, since its development proceeded in well-defined, discrete stages determined by the extensive marshes or fens south of the Charles River. The first development occurred on Beacon Hill, the high ground between the Charles River and Boston Harbour. It became the early fashionable area. Later the New South End was built, to the south of the fens, and later, when the flow of the river was contained and the swamp south of the river filled in, the Back Bay District was established. These three areas differ architecturally, and their cast iron ornamentation also varies.

Plates 239–250

The residential area of Beacon Hill was built between 1800 and 1850, largely on the declivity between the beacon and the Charles River. Fortunately it is almost unchanged and, because of enlightened legislation, should remain so. It includes Louisburg Square and streets running towards the river on the north-west – Pinckney, Mount Vernon and Chestnut Streets – with Beacon Street on the south bordering Boston Common. The early architecture had its inspiration in that of Georgian London: houses were mostly built in terraces, or rows, and (as in New York) they were given classical doorways to enrich their plain façades. The fabric is brick, with the wooden frames of the windows let into the brick. The façade might be flat, but more typically bows curve elegantly on each side of the recessed entrance doors. Iron fences mark the street line and border steps leading to the front door, while window guards or balustrades of iron adorn the balconies. As in London the balconies are usually open (without roofs) and confined to the first floor, which alone has French windows.

Plates 252–257

The New South End was built chiefly between 1851 and 1859, upon land south of the fens. Massachusetts Avenue, running southwards, skirted the west side of the great fen and inclined somewhat eastward below the marsh to enter the South End. It expanded into Chester Square and nearby are Worcester, Blackstone and Franklin Squares, the last two being separated by Washington Street.

Plate 253

The houses of the South End followed the Beacon Hill tradition, but differences are to be observed. Bows remain, with slightly recessed portals, which are raised high above street level and reached by flights of stairs flanked by cast iron railings which are often of *rinceau* design. The high level of the entrance floor, with a semi-basement below, caused the house to be set further back from the street so that a small garden plot with its own railings fronts the house. These railings often show Gothic patterns.

Neo-classical porticos were abandoned, possibly for reasons of economy, and the entrance doors are capped by curved lintels or by projecting hoods supported by heavy brackets. Window guards and balconies were rarely added, and the anthemion pattern is nowhere to be seen.

The neighbourhood was originally well-to-do, but by the 1880s slum-like conditions of overcrowding had become established behind the fine façades. However, at the time of photography some houses were being renovated (some for low-cost housing) and a battle for preservation had been joined.

Plates 258, 261

Between about 1860 and 1900 the large swamp south of the Charles River was filled in, to form the Back Bay District. The reclaimed area extended roughly between the Charles River on the north and Tremont Street on the south (above the New South End), with Massachusetts Avenue on the west and Old South End and Boston Common on the east.

This large area became available for building at a time when young architects, returning from studies in France, turned to the Second Empire for inspiration.

Thus the style gradually changed from Georgian, Regency and Victorian to something reflecting the Parisian formula. Individual houses were built in tall blocks of unified design bordering corridor-like streets. The cornices of different blocks match each other in height, thus giving uniformity to the appearance of the street. Mansard roofs are the rule. Brownstone and stucco are widely used, with archaeologically correct ornamentation. The window openings are set off from the façade by raised mouldings of stone or stucco, and a pediment or cornice gives importance to the ground floor windows. Fortunately cast iron ornamentation was not rejected, probably because it was characteristic of the boulevards of Paris. Its patterns also appear to have been influenced by Parisian designs. Iron-filled overdoors and cast iron panels in the entrance doors are a further reminder of French influence. However, ironwork is much less in evidence than in the other areas. A period of eclecticism followed during the years 1869–85, and this was in turn followed by a period of revivals, with the Georgian or Adam style, so prominent in the earlier years of the young developing city, predominating.

Plates 258, 261

The essential characteristics of the Back Bay are best seen in Commonwealth Avenue and the grid of streets on either side between Beacon and Boylston Streets.

Philadelphia, Pennsylvania

There is a very large amount of early wrought iron in the city, made by German craftsmen who came to Philadelphia. However, cast iron became common as large foundries were established. Iron ore was smelted in nearby Pittsburgh and a canal, constructed between the two cities in 1834, facilitated the transport of pig-iron to Philadelphia. Much of the ironwork of New Orleans, until the casting industry was established locally, was made in Philadelphia and transported down the Delaware River to the sea and thence up the Mississippi River to be landed at New Orleans. Many other cities were supplied by the foundries of Philadelphia.

Plates 263, 264
Plate 4
Plates 265, 266

Philadelphia is renowned for its vast and successful scheme of restoration and reconstruction of the mainly eighteenth-century neighbourhood known as Society Hill. The Bishop Stevens House illustrates the virtue of restoration. Its ironwork design appears in Cottingham's *The Smith and Founder's Director*, published in London in 1824. In contrast the lyre motif, ubiquitous in Philadelphia, is seen only once in very simple form in the thousands of patterns illustrated by Cottingham. A highly unusual use of cast iron occurs in the Philadelphia Hospital: iron Doric columns not only support the wards but also serve as ducts for hot air, so forming a useful heating system.

Baltimore, Maryland

Baltimore is especially noted for the spectacular Peabody Institute Library, and for the foundry which cast its ironwork, and much other domestic ironwork in Baltimore and elsewhere.

Plates 267–275

George Peabody, born in Massachusetts in 1795, began work as a grocer's apprentice at the age of 11 and eventually became one of the foremost financial experts and philanthropists of his time. His gifts and bequests to the Peabody

Institute, begun in 1857, amounted to $1,400,000. The library collection was designed to provide material for the study of all subjects except law and medicine.

The present library building was designed by E. G. Lind of Baltimore, and the structural material was iron, manufactured by Bartlett, Robbins & Co. of Baltimore. The specifications of the library, an addition to the Peabody Institute, were printed by William K. Boyle and Son of Baltimore in 1875. Amongst specifications for the ironwork that of the visible part was described as follows:

Plates 270, 271

Plate 267

IRON COLUMNS. — Provide and set where shewn on Basement plan, cast iron columns of approved design for support of the girders and beams of Library floor above. To have an external diameter of 9″, to be 1¾″ thick, and the bases and caps accurately turned to a true plane.

Cast iron plates on shoes 1½″ thick, to be provided and well bedded in cement on the brick piers for receiving said columns, with raised flanges and stubs to keep same in position. The caps to be fitted with similar plates and cast iron joint boxes, for receiving the columns above.

The columns shewn on plans of Library and story above, to be also of cast iron with ornamental caps, bases and fillets as shewn, bolted and secured to each other, so as to form a continuous column and support to roof. Those on lower story, to be 1¾″ thick, and those above diminishing in thickness, to the topmost series, which will be ⅞″ thick.

Each column to be fitted with flanges for receiving the iron beams and supports for book cases – and rivet holes punched into them for securing same.

The building was opened for public use on 1 October 1878, and it stands today as the builders left it except for the substitution of electric light for gas in 1892.

The library holds two small undated catalogues of the foundry which was described in *The Great Industries of the United States* (1872) as one of the best established works in the United States: the firm of Hayward, Bartlett & Co., which changed its name in 1866 to Bartlett, Robbins & Co. It could produce a house, all complete, with walls, floors, doors, windows, roofs, verandas, balconies, cornices and external ornamentation of all kinds. The catalogues show classical columns, pilasters, architraves, urns, fountains, chairs, tables, spittoons (small fancy 75 cents, loose top $1.50, large hotel size with hinged top $1.85), and irons, balusters, friezes, fringes, crestings for mansard or French roofs, etc.

Plates 268, 272

The history of the firm was traced by Ferdinand C. Latrobe, in *Iron Men and Their Dogs*, from Hayward & Friend in 1837 to the Koppers Company, Bartlett Hayward Division. Latrobe points out that the Corbett Building in Portland, Oregon, was manufactured about 1868 by Bartlett, Robbins & Co. and shipped round the Horn to Portland, a practice established at the time of the California Gold Rush to meet the urgent need for ready-made houses.

Plates 268, 269

Georgetown, Washington, D.C.

Georgetown began about 1730 as a group of wooden houses. Later it became a fashionable area with many fine brick houses adorned by Georgian doorways and classical pilasters. Classicism sometimes extended only to the portico, but sometimes symmetry and other details produced a Georgian impression. Older houses were refronted to conform to fashion, hence the area has an air of unity.

Plates 276–279

Ironwork abounds in the form of fences, steps and window guards. In the early houses the iron would be simply wrought; later, cast iron might be substituted. Balconies and cast iron porticos are rare. Characteristic of Georgetown are the cast iron steps leading from the sidewalk up to the raised doorways. Balusters, treads and risers are all of cast iron, the latter being pierced and patterned. The stairs may be straight or gracefully curved. Such stairs occur very occasionally elsewhere in the United States.

Plates 276, 278

Thus old Georgetown has a very special atmosphere displaying unostentatiously the grace of a past era to which ironwork makes an elegant contribution. Street lamps, illuminated by gas, add their charm. The area demonstrates the potency of civic pride and relentless determination in favouring conservation. Permission to effect even slight alterations must be obtained from the Fine Arts Commission, and if it is granted, check photographs must be supplied before work begins.

Charleston, South Carolina

Plates 280–288

Charleston, a southern port and county seat of Charleston County, is a serene city, with a leisurely pace. It is situated on a peninsula between two rivers and was originally a walled town, in which the houses were packed closely together, often a single room in width and set end-on to the street. This form, which played an important part in the development of the lateral veranda known locally as a 'piazza', was imposed upon the builders by the long narrow lots originally laid out in the 'Grand Modell' by the Lords Protector to whom Charles II granted this newly acquired land.

The houses were built of wood and followed English styles as closely as possible. With the passage of time the city was released from its early confines and wider blocks could be obtained. Conservatism determined the deep, narrow form of the house, while the increased width available allowed the construction of wide galleries along one side facing the garden. These galleries were a rational adaptation to the sultry climate, allowing cool outdoor living, catching whatever breeze there might be, and English planters returning from the West Indies may have favoured, or introduced, this modified veranda form. The piazzas are usually wide with classical columns, and usually several-storeyed. The house is entered from the piazza, through a doorway in the side at first-floor level.

Plate 280

In contrast are the large 'double houses' of symmetrical design with a more usual placement on the lot. The doorways are of Georgian design, while balconies or verandas may be simple or elaborate. Galleries may run across the width of the house, single or double-storeyed, and supported by classical columns which sometimes run the height of two storeys, after the manner of plantation houses. The entrance floor is often built up on an arcaded platform, as a protection against the moist terrain.

Plates 281, 282, 286, 287

The population has remained strongly anglophile, and the architecture and heirlooms of British origin play an important part in everyday life. Today many are intensely interested in their homes and intent on preservation. Poverty after the Civil War tended to preserve the old architecture, and with the affection for the old and the conservative distrust of 'progress' Victorian design is rare in the older parts of the city. The main periods are identified locally as Pre-Revolutionary (before 1783), Post-Revolutionary (1783–1812), and Ante-Bellum (1812–1860). An invaluable source is the remarkable little book *This is Charleston*, by Samuel Gaillard Stoney, published by the Carolina Art Association with the Historic Charleston Foundation and the Preservation Society of Charleston, which illustrates and briefly describes 572 buildings worthy of preservation. Some were destroyed between the two editions published in 1944 and 1960.

Plate 281

Smiths were plentiful in Charleston, but casting was little done. Hence wrought iron is commoner than cast, and was used until a later date than in other cities of the United States. However, there is some cast iron to be found, added after the Civil War. What there is blends well with the local architecture.

Plates 1, 286

New Orleans, Louisiana

New Orleans was founded by the French near the mouth of the Mississippi in 1718. The Spaniards, who governed the city between 1766 and 1801, left little lasting mark. The French were again in power after 1801, and though in 1804 the Louisiana Territory was sold by Napoleon to the young American Republic, French influence can still be felt in the city.

There are two distinct parts of New Orleans, the French Quarter or Vieux Carré, and the Garden District. The climate of the region is moist and hot, the ground marshy. These conditions are reflected in the architecture of both areas, and in the copious use of verandas and balconies. The early ironwork was wrought: cast iron came to be used after 1830. At first a combination of wrought and cast iron might be used, but soon cast iron predominated. Much of it was made in Philadelphia, some by the foundry of Wood and Perot, and sold by their New Orleans agent, Wood and Miltenberger. The castings were brought by water from Pennsylvania and it appears that most were added to houses after 1850. Later on, castings were made locally (see below, p. 47).

Plates 307, 308

The French Quarter has the form of an elongated rectangle lying along the Mississippi, with Jackson Square, containing the cathedral and former public buildings, at its centre. The houses, mostly rebuilt in brick after a disastrous fire in 1794, abut one on the other. The ground floor was used for business or domestic offices, and behind lay the kitchen and slave quarters. Also behind the houses, hidden from the street, are courtyards or patios, lush with tropical vegetation. Balconies with balustrades of wood, and occasionally of cast iron (later), overlook the courtyard. The windows facing the court come down to floor level, in the French manner, and the balconies served for outdoor living and external passageways. On the street fronts slender iron columns rise from the edge of the sidewalks to support one or two tiers of open or roofed balconies ('galleries') with finely designed castings. These wide galleries and broad eaves shade walls and windows.

Plates 289–303
Plate 291

Plates 292, 293, 298–300

Nowhere perhaps is there a closer liaison between climatic and environmental factors, local material (cypress wood and brick), temperament and architecture than in the French Quarter; and the Vieux Carré Commission is to be congratulated upon its work in preserving the district for the future. By the moral suasion of a citizens' committee and, if necessary, legal action, it has prevented demolition and alterations. The visitors are, and the future will be, grateful for their efforts. As a side issue, the commercial value of this preservation is very evident. Tourists pour into New Orleans and the stream will never cease – a lesson which should impress the practical-minded citizens of other areas, even if they have no interest in the cultural and aesthetic benediction which the past confers upon the present and the future.

Plates 304–317

In the Garden District one enters a different area. Originally a part of the Lafayette City area of New Orleans, it was peopled by well-to-do merchants who wanted space and gardens away from the unpleasant and even dangerous features of a waterside city (dreadful epidemics of cholera and yellow fever struck repeatedly, notably in 1832 and 1853). The first house of any consequence was built by Thomas Toby in 1838. Most are raised somewhat above ground level to avoid damp – the two-storey houses three or four feet, and the single-storey houses or 'raised cottages' as much as eight feet. Some are completely fronted with lacy ironwork, as in the Vieux Carré, but most combine iron-edged balconies or verandas with stuccoed columns in classical style.

Plates 311, 315
Plate 314
Plate 306
Plates 314, 315, 317

The history of the district is beautifully brought to life in *The Great Days of the Garden District and the Old City of Lafayette* by Martha and Ray Samuel (1961). The Samuels quote vivid contemporary impressions of the area, such as that in Julian Ralph's *Dixie, or Southern Scenes and Sketches*:

> . . . when I rode through the Garden District – the new part of the town – my lady friends pointed to the galleries and said: 'You should see them in the summer, before the people leave or after they come back. The entire population is out-of-doors in the air, and the galleries are loaded with women in soft colors, mainly white. They have white dresses by the dozen. They go about without their hats, in carriages and in street cars, visiting up and down the streets. In-doors, one must spend one's whole time and energy in vibrating a fan.

And Mark Twain, poet laureate of the Mississippi, observed that

> All the dwellings are of wood . . . and all have a comfortable look. Those in the wealthy quarter are spacious; painted snowy white, usually, and generally have wide verandas, or double-verandas, supported by ornamental columns. These mansions stand in the center of large grounds and rise, garlanded with roses, out of the midst of swelling masses of shining green foliage and many-colored blossoms. No houses could well be in better harmony with their surroundings, or more pleasing to the eye, or more home-like and comfortable-looking.

The writers are indebted to those who graciously permitted photography of their lovely homes.

Plate 321

The unique cemeteries of New Orleans also contain wrought and cast iron ornamentation, rich in the symbolism of death. The high water-table of the city called for above-ground burials, which became compulsory after 1800. Family vaults are usual, but there are also single tombs and large mausolea for groups or societies (the Lafayette Cemetery No. 1, for instance, contains a monument intended to accommodate all the members of a fire-engine company). The tombs assume architectural forms, and many are surrounded by iron railings. While wrought iron predominated in the early period, ornamental motifs were cast: they include urns and spent arrows, inverted torches, weeping willows and – perhaps incongruously – pineapples, symbols of welcome. The cemeteries have suffered from vandalism; when we visited the city only the St Louis Cemetery No. 2 remained open, but the situation has since improved.

When searching for foundries in New Orleans which made castings during the nineteenth century, Hinderer's Iron Works was discovered. The main ironworks was established in 1864; unfortunately in 1960 it was about to close – though it was still prepared to supply components for repairs or replacements. The introduction to Hinderer's American Institute of Architects file (1929) states:

Plate 304

> STEEPED in the glamor and tradition of the old south, cast verandahs by HINDERER'S IRON WORKS have graced the plantation homes and town houses of the most discriminating since the early days of the war between the states.
>
> The best tradition and design of old New Orleans cast iron lace work, is embodied in the patterns illustrated on the succeeding plates. These designs are not copies or adaptations of nineteenth century iron work, but are produced from original patterns, which have been in our possession for over three quarters of a century.

Early Hinderer catalogues, consisting of large folded sheets (96 × 83 cm) show a great variety of wares – fountains, drinking fountains (for men and dogs), flower boxes, boot-scrapers, settees, chairs, large animals, andirons, flower arches and frames, gates, fences, hitching posts and ornamental garden vases, some copyrighted in 1890. A catalogue of 'Garden Furniture and Lawn Requisites' published in 1931 depicts garden seats with grapevine, morning glory and fern leaf patterns (aluminium replicas of the latter are now available in several countries), a set of chairs with medallions representing the four seasons, and much else.

San Francisco and Columbia, California

The themes for San Francisco are demolition and preservation, and its cast iron buildings and façades, of which few now remain. Plate 323 shows the intact façade of the Trust Department of the American Trust Company, originally the London and San Francisco Bank, at the north-west corner of California and Leidesdorff, and plates 324 and 325 show its demolition in 1959. The American Institute of Architects had designated it as one of twelve outstanding San Francisco buildings that should be preserved. When it was replaced by a new headquarters building, the bank donated key sections of the structure to several public institutions: a small unit went to the Society of California Pioneers, the entire entrance was to be re-assembled at the San Francisco Maritime Museum, and an ornate window unit from the first floor was presented to the Oakland Municipal Art Museum for their 'Archives of California Art' section. (We are extremely grateful to the American Trust Company for supplying photographs and information, and for granting permission to reproduce the material.)

Plates 322–327

A number of cast iron façades in the Jackson Street area escaped damage during the earthquake and fire of 1906, among them the Hotaling liquor warehouse (now Kneedler-Fauchère Building) at Nos. 451–461 Jackson Street, which was in beautiful condition when we saw it. Its ground-floor columns bear the mark of the California Foundry, San Francisco. At No. 526 Washington Street, a cast iron colonnade made by the Vulcan Foundry Co. supports upper storeys of brick.

Plate 326

Another foundry is identified in the next-door building, whose plain pilasters are marked 'Sutter Iron Works, 1851'.

Plate 322

Probably the first cast iron front in the city, and undoubtedly one of the most splendid, was the Savings and Loan Society in Clay Street, built in 1870. Like the Haughwout Building in New York, it was designed by J. P. Gaynor, of whom little else is known. Long since vanished, the building is recorded in an early photograph which shows Ephraim W. Burr, President of the Savings and Loan Society and three-term mayor of San Francisco in the 1850s, standing in the doorway in a top hat.

San Francisco was a portal to the Mother Lode area of California: Columbia, about 150 miles away, is the most complete of the early gold-mining towns of that area, thanks to a decision by the State Legislature to preserve historic buildings and their setting and to encourage the survival of local community life.

By May 1852 (according to the guide published by the Department of Natural Resources, Division of Beaches and Parks),

> A large business district was built, and stores, saloons, gambling rooms, hotels, restaurants, churches, livery stables, bakeries, social and fraternal halls, banks and a variety of other establishments soon flourished.
>
> During the 1850s Columbia's population, including environs, was probably several thousand people . . .
>
> Fires destroyed a large portion of the town's business district on July 10, 1854. The frame buildings thus lost were quickly rebuilt, and this time more brick was used. Some of these brick buildings still stand. On August 25, 1857, fire again wiped out all the frame structures and numerous brick ones in an area of some 13 square blocks. Six men lost their lives in this disaster. Several brick structures which were saved from the flames, as well as some erected soon after the fire, are still in use. These buildings have large, double iron doors and window shutters, designed to prevent the spread of fire. These iron doors and shutters are characteristic of California's old mining towns.

Plate 328

It was interesting to find cast iron balustrades on the first floor balconies of a number of buildings. This would fit in with the period of restoration and rebuilding after the fire of 1857.

5 Australia and New Zealand

This section of the book may at first appear to be disproportionately long. However, Australia's cities were built up during the cast iron era, and their climate encouraged the lavish use of cast iron for balconies and verandas: Melbourne has more architectural cast ironwork than any other city in the world. And time and proximity have allowed an extensive study and more photography of ironwork in Australia.

Plates 381–416

The use of cast iron ornamentation was undoubtedly inspired by memories of the homeland, but in both usage and patterns it became more flamboyant than that of England. The mode of usage differed in the capital cities and a great variety of styles resulted, depending upon the date of settlement, the distance below the equator, the architecture in vogue at the time of expansion, the wealth of the community, the discovery of gold, the establishment of local foundries and the influence of fashion once a style was established.

The earliest settlements of New South Wales and Van Diemen's Land (Tasmania) began in the years 1788 and 1803 respectively. The earliest official buildings were designed by military architects and engineers, followed by civilian architects and builders, some of whom had been transported as convicts. Training, memory and the few architectural treatises available influenced the reproduction of simplified Georgian and Regency styles. Later, the builders felt the need for ornamentation of their plain façades, and so chose ironwork in remembrance of the cities with which they were familiar. Later still, Victorian influences gained sway (1837–1901), followed by Edwardian. It is convenient to use these terms based on the monarchy, although changes in the dominant architecture were slow and obviously could not be limited to the reign of a monarch. Trans-shipment of material and ideas to a colony was slow. Nomenclature of architectural types is difficult, classification being sometimes based on obscure differences or resemblances stretched to the limit, sometimes very far from the prototypes. For these reasons a simple classification is used. Such terms as Georgian, Regency, Neoclassical, Tudor, Gothic and Italianate can usually be understood. Art Nouveau had international significance.

Plates 456, 457

Plate 410

Georgian designs in Australia were simpler than those in England, and were marked in general by plain symmetrical façades. In a terrace the houses, as in England, had identical façades while the entrance was usually on one side of the front. The late Georgian or Regency style was somewhat more elaborate and

Plate 351
Figure 12

49

Plates 48, 358

Plate 395
Plates 393, 460

Plates 439, 440, 457

Plate 428

marked by bays and bows. The ironwork of Sydney on cantilever first-floor balconies with filigree columns was similar to London usage, while the Melbourne style is quite different. In terraces and houses built in Australia in the later part of the reign of Queen Victoria, the trim is usually coarse. Detached houses not infrequently have a square tower and some associated features which justify the term Italianate. Late Victorian and Edwardian houses broke away from the earlier limiting styles and in the latter asymmetry became a characteristic, often with many minor ornamental frolics.

It is usually stated that military architects who had served in the East brought the roofed 'colonial' veranda to Australia, but other sources are possible. Certainly the veranda and roofed balcony suited the sunny hot climate of the new land, especially on houses having a northerly aspect. The veranda, perhaps with a superimposed balcony, may run along two or three sides of a detached house, or completely surround a single-storey country house. The importance of aspect was not always understood, for the builder thought in terms of the northern hemisphere. There a north-facing balcony was unthinkable; but in Australia a balcony facing north would be penetrated by the low noonday sun in the winter, while the roof would protect rooms from the high sun in summer. Facing east, the roofing of veranda and balcony would not prevent access of morning sunshine; facing west, the roofing would not shield from the hot late afternoon sunshine of summer. Balconies on the southern aspect catch only early morning and late evening sunshine in summer-time. In general, roofed balconies and verandas face the streets, whatever the aspect, and thus sometimes they can serve only an ornamental or fashionable role.

Figure 12

Plates 395, 399

In the urban setting terraces of abutting houses were built, as in England, but rarely as long. At first simple cast iron was used to relieve the plain façades, but in later Victorian examples the façade and ironwork enter into more exuberant partnership. Superimposed pediments and parapets, using a multitude of decorative motifs, become very common in Melbourne.

Plates 359, 389

Usually of two, and occasionally of three storeys, the depth of terrace houses provided much internal space on a limited frontage. The dividing walls, extending to the edge of the veranda and balcony, give quiet and privacy which multi-storey modern housing estates cannot equal. The importance of a garden plot or courtyard, however small, can hardly be exaggerated as an adjunct to pleasant living. The sitting room is usually on the first floor front, where the ironwork of a sunny balcony provides an ever-changing shadow pattern and a pleasant foreground to the vista of parkland, street, and in Sydney of the harbour. Unfortunately views of the harbour have been eliminated by high-rise buildings.

Plate 367

The backs of individual terrace houses were L-shaped, in order to provide windows for a greater number of rooms. Hence the important rooms were usually in the front of the house. However, modern redesigning of the rear of the house usually provides a large ground floor room with a glass wall and access to an attractive courtyard or garden.

PROVENANCE OF THE CAST IRON ORNAMENTATION
It is constantly said that the ironwork of Australia came from England as ballast in sailing ships. Indeed this was, and often still is, the automatic response to any mention of ornamental cast iron. Like many legends it is untrue. Undoubtedly,

in the early stages some ornamental ironwork was imported from the United Kingdom, but careful packing as cargo would be necessary to prevent breakage. Some patterns have been recognized in Britain and in Australia, but even in these instances copies were later made in Australia. Castings were made in Australia before pig-iron was produced locally. Solid, heavy bars of pig-iron which could be used as ballast were imported and, after remelting, used for casting of ornamental ironwork, but this practice lessened when iron ore was smelted in Australia. Bars of wrought iron were probably also imported. The first smelting of iron ore in Australia was carried out at Mittagong (New South Wales) in 1848, but the high cost of obtaining and transporting suitable fuel was largely responsible for the difficulties encountered by the industry and its ultimate failure. In Victoria at Lal Lal a blast furnace smelted iron ore between 1875 and 1884, but failed for similar reasons.

Figure 5, Plate 414
Plates 431–436

On a wide fence post in Gawler, South Australia, is cast the following information:

> Cast from the first iron smelted in the Colony at the Phoenix Foundry 1871 from ore raised in the District of Barossa. Presented by James Martin Esq; J.P. Gawler 1876

The claim was obviously incorrect, due probably to poor communication. Amongst Miscellanea in the *History of Gawler 1837–1903* the following appears:

> From the 'Bunyip' of November 9, 1872:—This week we have the highly gratifying intelligence to communicate that Messrs. Martin & Co., of the Phoenix Foundry, have experimented successfully upon the smelting of our native ores. We yesterday visited the firm's new foundry and had the satisfaction of seeing turned out of the moulds, of excellent quality, cog wheels, ploughshares, a medallion portrait, looking glass frame, handsome picture frame, and various other articles, including a tea cup with saucer and teaspoon. The fact is thus established that we shall be able to rear up and multiply metallic pigs to any extent. Messrs. M. & Co. are now constructing the necessary appliances for a movement on an enlarged scale, Barossa supplying both the iron ore and the charcoal, and we need hardly say that the realisation of this great desideratum must prove of vast importance to those interests of the colony, which we would not expect to enumerate fully at present if we made the attempt.

Another paragraph, obviously referring to a later date, states (p. 354):

> The late Mr James Martin hoped that iron ore would be successfully smelted here. There are large deposits of the material, but, unfortunately, coal has to be brought from a great distance, and this renders the process an unprofitable one. In the late seventies Mr Martin tried what could be done, but while the smelting was a success the cost was too great.

Fowles in his fascinating *Sydney in 1848* mentions that

> At the back of Messrs. Harper and Moore's, is the Sydney Foundry, an extensive establishment belonging to the Messrs. Russell.

It is probable that the foundry produced its castings from imported pig-iron.

REGISTRATION OF DESIGNS

At first simple, the patterns gradually acquired complexity, but usually remained pleasing. Most of the patterns were founded on traditional motifs. The designer of cast iron in Australia, coming late in the history of decoration, was eclectic.

Plate 329

In Australia designs could be officially registered for copyright purposes. In New South Wales 23 foundries registered 103 designs for ornamental ironwork, the earliest being on 17 December 1879. After the end of the century many other

Plate 332

utilitarian objects were registered. In Victoria 38 foundries registered 161 designs, the earliest on 8 April 1870 being a frieze showing a nesting swan as the central motif of a flowing *rinceau* design. The last registration was dated 20 August 1900.

Plate 335
Plate 338

In South Australia 29 designs were registered between 4 March 1880 and 27 February 1885, most being for gates and fences. In Queensland 8 foundries registered 74 patterns between November 1885 and November 1902. In a number of instances the same design was registered in two states by different firms.

The date of registration is not an automatic indication of the date of manufacture of a particular pattern or of the building bearing it, for registration may have occurred long after the design was initiated, and a pattern would be available for years after registration.

It will be noted that, save in a few instances, registration of ornamental castings ceased at the end of the nineteenth century. Designs in pressed steel were then appearing, to be used in sheets chiefly for ceilings.

Some registered designs are shown in plates 329, 332, 335 and 338; but many of the originals were too poor for reproduction. The plates are illustrated because in rapid view they show the essence of Australian design, and it may please some to recognize designs shown in subsequent illustrations of houses.

The names of many other foundries have been found.

CATALOGUES

*Plates 330, 331, 333, 334,
336, 337, 339, 433,
Figures 8–10, 13, 14*

Catalogues of local firms provide clearer pictures of their many designs. Fortunately, three very good catalogues, and a few minor ones, have survived. Outstanding are those of William Stephens's Excelsior Foundry at Melbourne and the 'Sun' Foundry of A. C. Harley & Co. at Adelaide.

INDIGENOUS DESIGNS

Plates 340–343

Plates 391, 442

Although distinctive, the motifs used were much the same as in other countries. However, most fascinating are indigenous patterns embodying Australian fauna and flora. Several patterns in plate 332 show registered indigenous designs, including fern patterns which are recognizably Australian. The number of fern patterns in Australian ironwork is interesting, for the fern is not a common motif elsewhere, except on cast iron chairs and seats. D. E. Allen in *The Victorian Fern Craze* (1969) states that a popular interest in ferns in England reached its zenith in the 1850s. The indoor use of ferns for decoration and prestige, with many methods of display, brought into use a popular language of its own. Growing many different varieties of ferns from spores gave a somewhat scientific flavour to indoor gardening in glass cases and in ferneries, while outdoor excursions to hunt for specimens became a popular and healthful hobby. It would be strange if some of this craze did not spread to Australia, as did so many other Victorian fashions in the decorative arts. Another influence, and probably a more potent one, was

Figures 8, 9 Designs for balusters, friezes, brackets and narrow spandrels from the catalogue of William Stephens's *Excelsior Foundry, Melbourne, 1901. The 'Aesthetic' baluster no. 15 will be seen in pl. 394; spandrel no. 1 matches the baluster in pl. 387, and no. 3 with its patriotic crown matches the frieze in pl. 406. Note the ferns in spandrel no. 2, and the lovebirds in no. 7. Other parallels between these illustrations and designs registered or advertised by other firms, as well as actual castings, will be noticed: see, for instance, pls. 329, 330, 332, 336.*

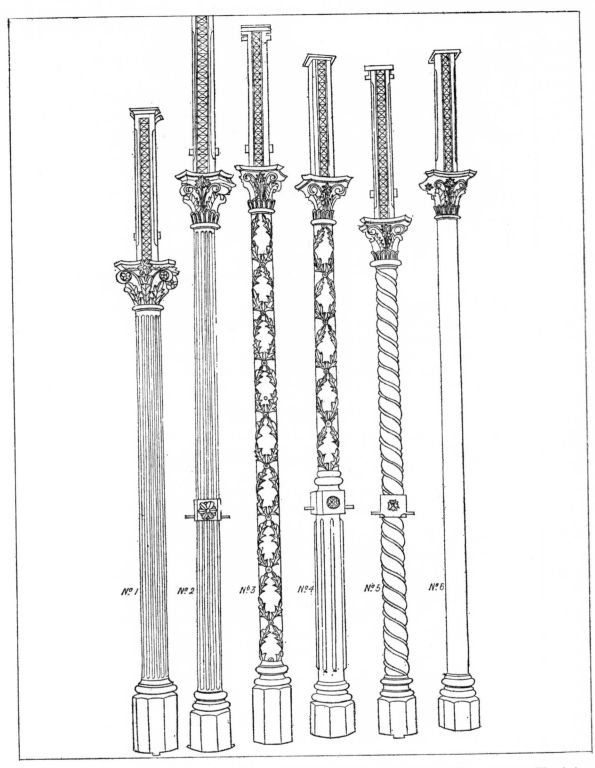

Figure 10   Veranda columns, from the catalogue of Stephens's Excelsior Foundry, Melbourne, 1901. The designs show various Corinthian capitals and ornamented shafts; the extensions at the top are slotted to received projections in the frieze, brackets and spandrels. For the method of casting columns, see p. 12.

the fascination exerted by the fern gullies in Australia. The early Australian poets found inspiration in the peace and beauty of the Australian bush, and it is not entirely fanciful to think that the indigenous plants of the fern gullies inspired craftsmen as well, so that the naturalistic fern became more recognizable than the highly stylized acanthus leaves of antiquity.

The kangaroo and the kookaburra, with its unbird-like laugh and ability to swallow small snakes, must have impressed people from abroad while emu, cassowary and aborigine indubitably seized the imagination of the early discoverers and later inspired the designers to capture their likenesses in cast iron. A curious case is that of a remarkable cast iron hallstand which displays native fauna and flora against backgrounds of indigenous ferns. Aboriginal masks are centred in trophies of weapons, fish and fowl. It was assumed that the hallstand was of Australian design and manufacture. However, on the reverse side a British registration mark gives the date 22 November 1864 (the first numeral of the day of the month is uncertain but the rest is very clear). It is also marked 'N.° 14 L', suggesting, as does its rarity, a limited edition. Unfortunately there is no indication of the maker's name. The matter is complicated by the two supporting brackets, showing cassowaries and kangaroos, which were registered in Victoria by J. McEwan & Co. on 20 January 1886 (see the lower two patterns in the fourth column of plate 332). It is probable that these were cast using the English brackets as patterns. If so, it is possible that some complete hallstands were reproduced in Australia. The English date is twenty-two years earlier than the Australian, hence it is improbable that the hallstand was first made in Australia and then copied in England.

Plates 341–343

The reasons suggesting the common production of castings in Australia may be briefly summarized:

(i)   The earliest record of casting columns in Australia was provided by Fowles (1848). The columns of the Congregational Church, Pitt Street, Sydney, 'were cast by Mr. Dawson, of Sydney, in a very neat and superior manner, and are the first series of ornamental columns cast in the Colony'. The church was built between 1841 and 1846.
(ii)   A record of a law suit which was joined in Sydney on 16 February 1887 gave an indication of competing manufacturers (see *The Australasian Ironmonger*, II, no. 4, 1 April 1887, pp. 84, 85).
(iii)   More important still, the law suit drew attention to the registration of patterns for copyright. This led us to a search for the original records, which were found in the Designs Office, Department of Patents, Commonwealth of Australia, Canberra. The records are only of designs which manufacturers chose to register and are no indication of the wealth of designs, nor of the number of manufacturers.
(iv)   Six catalogues of Australian manufacturers have been found. Probably other catalogues remain to be discovered.
(v)   In some instances the manufacturer's name is found on his castings.
(vi)   Most patterns incorporating Australian fauna and flora were designed and cast in Australia.
(vii)   Some wood patterns, carved for moulding, still exist.
(viii)   It will be shown subsequently that ironwork made in Britain was exported to Australia and subsequently copied in Australia.

Plates 377, 431
Plates 340–343

Plates 447, 448

Portable buildings in Australia

This work deals with castings added to the essential architecture of a building, serving both practical and ornamental functions. In this chapter a few examples of portable (prefabricated) iron buildings, imported into Australia from Great Britain, will be mentioned. In these iron was part of the essential structure of the building, while sometimes contributing a decorative element as well.

Prefabrication has become a subject of intense academic interest recently. The earliest portable buildings, in the last decade of the eighteenth century and the early part of the nineteenth century, were made of wood. Most of those imported into Australia were made in Great Britain to answer the early colonist's profound need for protection from the hostile climatic conditions. Similarly, in America, portable buildings were produced for the pioneers spreading into new regions. It would be reasonable to suppose that some of these came to Australia. Professor Gilbert Herbert has made a study of Manning's Portable Colonial Cottages, which were cheap and easily erected and, although not ideal residences, were infinitely better than tents and locally made shelters. Loudon in *An Encyclopaedia of Cottage, Farm, and Villa Architecture* (1833) gives a fascinating account and illustrates the construction of 'A Portable Cottage for the Use of Emigrants and others'. He indicates that a flue of iron piping running horizontally from the cast iron stove through the various rooms might suffice to heat the whole house. In hot weather a simple valve would direct smoke into a vertical chimney.

Such wooden cottages could supply the demand for houses created by the gold rushes of Australia and California; however by that time the new technology of iron prefabrication was beginning to replace wooden constructions. The ability to make large corrugated sheets, later protected from rusting by a coating of zinc (galvanizing) made possible large, imposing and durable building of iron.

Many portable iron buildings were imported into Australia, especially into Victoria, when after the discovery of gold the population of Melbourne increased very rapidly. In Melbourne building materials and builders were very scarce, and all artisans who were able left the city in search of gold. The merchant Edward Keep wrote reminiscently in *The Australasian Ironmonger* for 1 November 1899: 'The profit on some transactions in those days seems now almost incredible . . . I had sent out to me 70 "houses" complete, costing me £25 each landed. These readily sold at auction by Symons & Perry at £60 or £70 each.' No doubt many prefabricated buildings were of such a miserable type that their eventual removal was welcomed, but some early iron portable houses are still to be found in Melbourne. Dr Miles Lewis of the School of Architecture, University of Melbourne, has studied prefabrication in fascinating detail and the expanded material of his thesis should soon be published. A certain amount of material based on photographic discoveries was published in *Victorian Heritage* (1960) and will be the basis of this chapter.

The demand for buildings encouraged English designers to supply not only prefabricated dwellings but large buildings as well. *The Illustrated London News* of 30 April 1853 depicts one such church sent to Australia. Part of the accompanying letterpress applies to portable buildings in general.

'Nothing like iron' is one of the most practical 'modern instances'. The employment of iron may be traced through a long vista of ages; but it was reserved for our generation to produce the iron bridge, the iron road, the iron ship, and the iron house; and within the last few months towns of iron houses, to shelter the hordes of emigrants to newly-discovered lands of gold. A remarkable instance of the new manufacture, and its rapid extension, to meet the demands caused by the exodus to South Australia, has largely occurred in the city of Bristol, at Clift-house, Bedminster, where the stock of galvanized iron houses for emigrants has increased in a comparatively short time from a single model cottage to a sufficient number of dwellings in progress to form a little town; besides stores, villas, an hotel, parsonage-houses for missionaries; and, last of all, a church, which has been ordered by the right rev. the Lord Bishop of Melbourne, and which it is believed is only the first of several which will be sent out to supply the means of public worship to the diggers. The smallest house made is the 'cottage for the million'. It comprises two neat rooms, measuring 16 feet by 12, and can be purchased as low as 35 guineas. A house, in course of completion for the auditor of Melbourne, comprises four rooms, of 14 feet square, with an entrance-hall, closets, and a detached kitchen, and fitted with venetian blinds to every window, and a verandah running all round the villa. A parsonage-house has been made at a cost of 250 guineas, to the order of the Bishop of Melbourne; it contains a sitting-room, kitchen, servants room, store-room, pantry, and four bed-rooms. The hotel or lodging-house is to comprise fourteen bed-rooms, so constructed as to divide into four compartments each, thus enabling the occupier to make up fifty-six beds.

The Argus of 3 September 1853 contains the following news item from Liverpool:

IRON CHURCH FOR MELBOURNE. — A short time since we gave a description of an iron church, intended for Australia, and which has attracted considerable attention, at the works of Mr Hemming, the eminent contractor of Bristol, who has also an establishment at Birkenhead. We may now add, that the church has been built under the order of the Bishop of Melbourne, and forms the first of nine or ten which are intended to be sent out.

The iron buildings were to have practical disadvantages such as the cost of erection, often far exceeding the cost of the material, and insulation insufficient to cope with a hot summer. The *Dictionary of Architecture* of the Architectural Publications Society of London (1853–92) has the following entry:

Iron — for Australia, and other places where builders and building materials are scarce, the invention of portable *iron houses* seemed to meet a temporary emergency. It is found, however, from their conducting power, that both heat and cold are insupportable in them. The expense of erection is also at times exorbitant. A merchant who took out to Melbourne an iron store, which cost £180, had to pay £700 for its erection, the wages of mechanics at the time being enormous . . .

Churches, have also been largely erected, by Hemming of the Clift House portable building manufactory, Bow [Bristol], for any required number of persons . . .

Further evidence that these churches were unsatisfactory is to be found in *The*

Church in Victoria during the Episcopate of the Right Reverend Charles Perry (Melbourne, 1892). George Goodman writes:

> The structure . . . was intended for Williamstown, but was by mistake consigned to Melbourne, thus entailing the needless expense of conveying it several miles up the Yarra and bringing it back to its proper destination. Then again as a building packed in fifty or sixty packing cases is somewhat more intricate than a child's dissected map, care ought to have been taken to send proper working drawings, or else an expert from the building-yard to superintend the process of erection. These necessary steps, unfortunately, were omitted, to the great vexation not only of the Williamstown parishioners but of the bishop himself. The sole merit of these buildings was their cheapness, and as a builder could not be sent from Bristol without entailing considerable expense, the neglect to do so was excusable, but the absence of working drawings admitted of no justification.
>
> Moreover, the colonists had ample reason for disliking these buildings. They are hot, ugly and perishable. The scorching sun draws the nails, curls the iron-plates, and makes the interior as hot as a baker's oven. The style of architecture is hopelessly unpleasing, and such as suggests the factory or the warehouse. It cannot therefore excite surprise that one parish after another declined these corrugated makeshifts. In several instances the idea was entertained, appeals were issued for subscriptions, and after all the expenditure of effort and raising of hopes, the imported church was left on the bishop's hands.

In spite of the cost of erection, the manufacturers of portable houses conducted a thriving trade. More attention was given to insulation.

The Baillieu Library, University of Melbourne, possesses a rare portfolio of illustrations, published by Hemming's Manufactory, styled *Patent Improved Portable Houses* and dealing with prefabricated buildings largely for the Australian trade. The following is extracted from a loose leaf inserted into the portfolio:

> The erections are entirely put together with iron screws, and completely erected at the works previous to shipment, and may be re-erected by any inexperienced person in a few hours, every part having been carefully fitted, numbered, and lettered; descriptive plans being given with every building.
>
> Every description of DWELLING HOUSES, STORES, SHOPS, WARE-HOUSES, CHURCHES, CHAPELS, SCHOOL-ROOMS, of any dimensions, to any given Plans, may be constructed in a few days ready for Shipment, delivered free alongside in Bristol, or at the Bristol Railway Stations.
>
> AN EMIGRANT POPULATION WITHOUT LODGINGS: THE EVIL AND ITS REMEDY. By a recent Visitor, Reprinted from the 'Lady's Newspaper.' MIGRATION may be of two sorts; – the one a reckless and ignorant desire of change, full of present discomfort, and ending most commonly in expectations disappointed and feelings disgusted; – the other, the calm determination of sober reflection, that weighs its peculiar difficulties, and wisely sets itself to the task of overcoming them. The one class of Emigrants are like the Tourists who would go forth on a long journey unprovided with umbrella or great coat, because the sun shone when they set out; the others are the careful

travellers, who have these appliances carefully folded up and stowed away for use when wanted.

It should never be forgotten by the Emigrant that he is going from a country of cheap labour, to a land where labour is dear; and this, which is one of the main inducements to Emigration, should lead him to provide at home those indispensable necessaries which he must otherwise procure, at whatever cost, on his arrival. Among the first of these necessaries we must surely reckon a shelter – a home; and though in a climate like Australia, we may take liberties which elsewhere would be fatal, yet it is wise to recollect, that even to the healthy and vigorous man, a fit of sickness and long season of debility is too often the penalty he pays for determining to 'knock along somehow,' to say nothing of the exorbitant price which the meanest pig-sty commands as rent, and which soon exhausts a deeper purse than would have supplied a comfortable home for the stranger, keeping him both in health and spirits.

A prefabricated theatre of some grace, made in England by Messrs Bellhouse and Co., has unfortunately long since been destroyed, but it is described in *The Year-Book of Facts in Science and Art* (London, 1855):

THEATRE. — Messrs. Bellhouse and Co. have also constructed a complete iron shell and framework of a spacious portable theatre, for Mr George Coppin, who has engaged Mr G. V. Brooke, the tragedian, to perform in the principal towns in Australia. This complete portable theatre of iron, with all fittings and appurtenances, will cost a sum exceeding £4,000. The building constructed by Messrs. Bellhouse is 88 feet in length, 40 feet wide, and about 24 feet high from the ground level to the peak of roof. As the floor level of the pit will be sunk about five or six feet below the ground level, there will be considerable altitude in the interior. The walls are of cast iron, uprights (Bellhouse's patent), and galvanized corrugated iron sheets, No. 18, wire gauge. The roof consists of strong iron principals, having the galvanized sheets bolted thereupon. To the gable end of the building, which forms the front, is attached an ornamental building, arranged as box and pit offices, lobbies, and entrances. A degree of ornamental effect is given to this façade. The pit is very spacious, extending back from the foot-lights to the wall below the boxes to about 54 feet, and being 59 feet across. The gallery for the boxes projects 24 feet from the wall opposite the stage, and 8 feet from the wall on each of the sides of the theatre. This gallery is supported on iron columns and strong framework of timber. Messrs. Bellhouse undertook the complete shell of the building, the ornamental façade, and the principal framework of the interior, and engaged to have the whole on board ship in London in about thirty days from date of contract.

The populace called the theatre the 'Iron Pot'.

ORNAMENTED PORTABLE BUILDINGS
There are two examples of domestic buildings which have special structural and ornamental qualities.

The present Tintern, Tintern Avenue, Toorak, Victoria, has a large iron portion with a bow window erected in 1854–55. The painted iron exterior is now visually indistinguishable from later additions of conventional materials made in 1895. The veranda is also a later addition. The manufacturers were Messrs W. and P. Maclellan of Glasgow.

Plates 345–350

By far the most ornate and interesting of cast iron dwellings in Australia is Corio Villa, Geelong, Victoria. We first became aware of the priceless importance of the cast ironwork of Corio Villa in 1958. During photography the present owner, Mr M. McAllister, referred us to a thesis on the villa submitted in 1949 to the School of Architecture, University of Melbourne, by Mr G. E. Drinnan. Mr Drinnan, now an architect in Geelong, was kind enough to allow his monograph to be included in *Victorian Heritage*. He wrote:

> Late in 1855 there was unloaded at the Cunningham pier (Geelong), a shipment of strange cast iron sections, classic vases, and roofing iron, a consignment from Glasgow with no particulars of sender or receiver.

Apparently the 'pieces' were shipped by some gentleman who had decided to settle in Geelong, and aware of the shortage of materials in the now flourishing community, he decided to export his own house from the newly set up prefabricating foundry in Glasgow, and erect it on his arrival. For six months this non-descript collection of building materials lay on the wharf unclaimed, and the port authorities began to make enquiries. These investigations proved fruitless, however, insomuch that the would-be immigrant could not be traced, and furthermore, the foundry, the 'alma mater' of the materials, had been destroyed by fire soon after its initial production, and all the moulds were destroyed; hence plans for erection were not forthcoming and the resultant 'Corio Villa' is certainly unique in Australia and possibly unique in the world.

Nothing remained but for the port authorities to dispose of these relics which were cluttering up their wharf, and they were eventually sold to Mr. Alfred Douglass for a small sum.

The iron sections were hauled to the top of the slope to a site overlooking the bay, where certain ingenious colonial craftsmen succeeded in solving the jig-saw puzzle without plans or directions.

The walls are prefabricated from $\frac{1}{2}$ inch cast iron boiler plate in 3 feet × 3 feet sheets but welded together to form wall sections complete with window openings. Internal linings are of lath and plaster. Sashes are solid cast iron which slide into broad corrugated English roofing iron which, after over ninety years service is quite weather-proof, and iron eaves gutters still carry roof water to the drains.

Plates 347, 348

Verandah posts and porch supports are cast in the most delicate filigree guilloche patterns, and one marvels at the facility of the craftsmen responsible for this ornamental work, for filigree is essentially the product of a more sympathetic material than cast iron. Most of the decorative work echoes the pattern of the rose, and the thistle of Scotland, but there are about eight classic vases of delightful proportions which serve as decorative flower pots on the sun porches and about the house.

Plates 348, 350

These sun porches are of exquisite design and are carried out in the same filigree cast iron.

Mr. Douglass had a cast iron replica of his family crest made and for many years it was fixed above the front porch. *Plates 346, 350*

The lion's head motif is repeated as a 'keystone' to each arch in verandahs and porches and strikes a note of kingly grandeur.

Barge boards are likewise of cast iron delicately patterned in fretwork, an attractive oriel vent in gable provides ventilation to roof space. *Plate 347*

A late Victorian addition was grafted on to the north-eastern end of the house in 1890. The portico, with wooden columns, suggested an addition, while the long veranda on the western side had obviously been filled in. That these assumptions were correct was shown by a photograph taken in 1875. The infill has now been removed. *Plate 349*
Plate 350

Plate 345

The history of the house is fascinating. It closely involves three men – the manufacturer of the component parts, the man who ordered the material and was responsible for its arrival in Australia, and finally, the man who subsequently bought the pieces and put them together into a home in which lived four generations of his family. The first two men remained unknown until recently. It is therefore reasonable to deal with the last man, whose name, Alfred Douglass, was known, and return to the other two later.

Mrs Clara Jones kindly provided the following historical information. The handwritten autobiography of Alfred Douglass, part of which follows, was copied by her sister, Mrs E. M. Sampson (*née* Douglass). It is remarkable that these two are granddaughters of Alfred Douglass who was born in 1820. Mrs Clara Jones (widow of Robert Chomley) and her son (George Alec Chomley, born 1922) lived at Corio Villa between 1923 and 1938 with her father H. P. Douglass, son of Alfred. The initial part of the autobiography is worth quoting as the background of Alfred Douglass who erected Corio Villa.

I, Alfred Douglass, the youngest son of James and Clarissa Douglass, was born at Loughborough, Leicestershire, England on the 14th March 1820. In 1825 my father removed to Doveridge, Derbyshire and there resided upon his estate.

Alfred was educated at a number of private schools and finally left school in June 1834 (aged 14). His biography continues:

On the 9th Nov 1834 I embarked on board the barque 'Wave', Captain Goldsmith, and sailed for Hobart Town, Van Diemen's Land, which port I reached on 9th March 1835 (aged 15) and became an inmate of the family of my relative Mr C. T. Smith and on 14th March 1835 I entered his office at a salary of £40 a year and resided with his family. . . .

I continued in the employ of Mr Smith till the 1st May 1850 (aged 30) when I determined to seek my fortune in Victoria. I embarked from Launceston and came over in the steamer Shamrock, Capt. Gilmore, in May 1850 and after remaining for a month in Melbourne and making an extended excursion to the westward . . . and another to the northward I determined to settle in Geelong and purchased some land below the Breakwater and erected my wool washing establishment and called it Barwonside . . . In Sept. 1851 gold was discovered in Victoria which shortly wrought a complete change in the prospects of this colony.

In the beginning of 1852 I made two excursions to Adelaide, South Australia, taking with me gold dust. The S. A. Government were then smelting the gold and it realised a higher price in that colony than Victoria. I purchased general merchandize which I consigned to Melbourne. Mr Richard Gibbs of Geelong joined me in these adventures which were highly remunerative. On March 3rd 1853 I married Elizabeth De Little of Launceston. The wedding breakfast was at the residence of her brother Robert De Little – her parents both being dead. In 1854 I erected my stores on Victoria Terrace. In 1854 our first child was born which died in infancy and in this year, 1854, my brother in law, Mr Joseph De Little, joined me in partnership the name of our firm being A. Douglass and Co. In 1855 I was made a magistrate and also a director of the London Chartered Bank. In 1856 I erected my residence 'Corio Villa' on Victoria Parade and we gave our house warming Nov. 10th 1856. Other children were born to us but it pleased God to call them away in infancy.

Plate 344

An intensive search for the provenance of the house in Australia and in the United Kingdom by Alfred Douglass's descendants had proved fruitless. While at Edinburgh in 1969 one of us met Mr (now Dr) Malcolm Higgs, who was then writing a thesis on prefabrication at the Department of Architecture of Edinburgh University. He was interested to know whether a plate in *Illustrations of Iron Structures, for Home and Abroad*, manufactured by Charles D. Young & Co. of Edinburgh, corresponded to the Corio Villa which he had seen reproduced in *Victorian Heritage*. The legend in the Edinburgh catalogue read:

Figure 14 is referred to as an excellent example of a Country Villa, in a neat style of architecture, with Verandas to correspond. The Villa, from which this is a drawing as actually erected, was made for the late Mr Gray, Colonial Land Commissioner at Geelong.

Knowing Corio Villa, it was possible to confirm Mr Higgs's suspicion. Certain alterations had been made, chiefly in the placing of one of the bowed porches, and in the type of columns used on the long western veranda.

It seemed that 'the late Mr Gray, Colonial Land Commissioner at Geelong', was William Nairn Gray, who was appointed Commissioner Portland Bay District on 1 July 1851. His death notice appeared in *The Argus* of 17 June 1854, and reveals that he died at Hamilton on 11 June 1854. It is little wonder that he failed to claim his villa.

The introduction of Young's *Illustrations of Iron Structures, for Home and Abroad*, typical of those of other iron founders of the day, throws some light on the virtues of his cast iron buildings, and the defects of the great majority of iron houses produced by others:

MANY inquiries having of late been addressed to Messrs C. D. YOUNG & CO., relative to Iron Buildings suitable for Warehouses, Stores, Markets, Arcades, Dwellings, Churches, Roofing, Sheds, &c., it is deemed advisable to publish the present Pamphlet, containing examples and descriptions of erections made of Iron applicable to these purposes. As a material for Building, Iron has long been greatly employed; and so much are its undoubted merits appreciated, that even in this Country, where there is no lack of stone or brick, and labour-work can be obtained at a comparatively moderate cost, it is in continued and increasing demand. But while hitherto only used as an auxiliary, Iron now bids fair to become the principal material employed – buildings of a high class of architecture, as well as of plain design, being constructed entirely of it. This is not surprising when its many advantages are considered. Of these may be enumerated – the small extent of ground-surface taken up by the walls – their imperviability to damp or moisture – the shortness of time occupied in construction – the practicability of rendering the building completely fire-proof – its being immediately occupiable without the serious drawback of damp walls – the ease and comparatively small cost of removal and recon-struction elsewhere – and the great facilities naturally afforded for the complete and thorough ventilation of the structure. Besides, an Iron House is necessarily much stronger than one constructed of other materials, from the facility with which, by the substitution of malleable iron in place of timber for the joisting, the walls and floors can be framed and effectually bound together, thereby giving a rigidity as well as strength to the whole building unattainable by any other means. So much so is this found to be the case, that this system of joisting is daily becoming more generally adopted, here and abroad, in the erection of both Government and Private Buildings.

The examples C. D. YOUNG & CO. have given in the subjoined Engravings are merely a selection of such structures as have in various parts of the world actually been erected; but they will be sufficient to convey an idea of the character of this class of work, and at the same time the importance of the subject is evidenced in the peculiar and varied adaptability of this system to all required forms and purposes, and needs only greater publicity to be justly appreciated.

The great majority of Iron Houses which have been constructed in this country and sent abroad, are by no means to be taken as criterions in forming a correct judgment of the merits of the system; as these structures, at least so far as regards Dwelling-houses and Stores, have, for the most part, been mere shells of sheet-iron, often neither wind nor water tight, and quite unadapted to resist either heat or cold, notwithstanding the fact that iron offers the greatest facilities for the accomplishment of these objects.

Further confirmation, if any were needed, of the manufacturer of Corio Villa came from a book in our possession entitled *A Short Treatise on the System of Wire Fencing, Gates, Etc. as Manufactured by Charles D. Young & Company*, printed in Edinburgh in 1850. The second half of the book is an *Illustrated and Descriptive Catalogue of Ornamental Cast and Wrought Iron and Wire Work*, and here the two types of urn found at Corio Villa appear. The urns on the bowed porches are of the pattern which Young calls the 'Medici Vase', a pattern shown a generation earlier in Cottingham's *Smith and Founder's Director*, published in London in 1824.

Plate 350

It is of further interest that the anthemion-patterned railing on the late Victorian addition to Corio Villa is shown as 'Balcony Railing from Upper Woburn Place' in Henry Shaw's *Examples of Ornamental Metal Work*, published in London in 1836.

Plate 349

Plate 12

Charles D. Young's *Illustrations* also allowed recognition of the birthplace of St Stephen's Presbyterian Church, Sydney. The church was demolished and put together again to serve as recreation hall and chapel of the Lidcombe State

Figure 11 'Iron Dwelling House with Shop below. With handsome cast iron front constructed by Charles D. Young and erected in Collins Street, Melbourne.' From Illustrations of Iron Structures, for Home and Abroad, *published by the foundry of Charles D. Young & Co. of Edinburgh* c. *1855. (Reproduced by courtesy of the Royal Institute of British Architects, London)*

Hospital and Home, New South Wales, but unhappily it was finally demolished and sold as scrap iron.

Young's *Illustrations of Iron Structures* refers to one other building for Australia: a shop erected for Messrs Miller & Dismor in Collins Street, Melbourne, said to have been largely of cast iron, and to have been 'the first building of the kind sent out to Australia', and 'one of the handsomest shops in Melbourne'. The building was demolished so many years ago that it cannot be traced.

Figure 11

St Luke's Church of England, Whitmore Square, Adelaide, South Australia, is a combination of a mutilated ironwork church and masonry. The unusual history is given in the centenary booklet of the church. It now reads like a comedy of errors, but it was serious at the time.

In December 1853 the Bishop of Adelaide, who was then in England, was requested to buy an iron church which would hold at least 450 persons. At a meeting of subscribers in April 1854,

> a letter was read from the Bishop, stating that as an iron Church would cost £2,000 (exclusive of expenses), he thought it inexpedient to purchase such a Church and advised against doing so. Special meetings were then held and it was decided to proceed with a stone one, and Mr E. Wright was appointed Architect.
>
> Unfortunately, the Bishop, after the despatch of his letter, gave orders for the iron Church to be built and forwarded, and the foundations of the new Church had been put in when the Church arrived. This iron Church, however, on arrival, was condemned by Lloyd's Agent. To further add to the complication, the Church had not been properly insured; the first monies subscribed were, therefore, practically thrown away. However, the present structure was proceeded with, fresh subscriptions came in, and part of the iron Church was used in the building as it now stands, the remainder being sold.

The church still stands with a front of stone, but with a considerable amount of imported iron, chiefly of corrugated type, used on the sides and roof.

Sydney, New South Wales

A despatch from Governor Phillip to Secretary of State Lord Sydney on 15 May 1788 reads:

> We got into Port Jackson early in the afternoon, and had the satisfaction of finding the finest harbour in the world . . .
>
> The different coves were examined with all possible expedition. I fixed on the one that had the best spring of water, and in which the ships can anchor so close to the shore that at a very small expense quays may be made at which the largest ships may unload.
>
> This cove, which I honoured with the name of Sydney, is about a quarter of a mile across at the entrance, and half a mile in length.

The early buildings were necessarily primitive and frail. As the colony developed, military and convict architects soon added attractive buildings. By the time cast iron ornamentation arrived in Sydney, corresponding with expansion of the

Plate 351

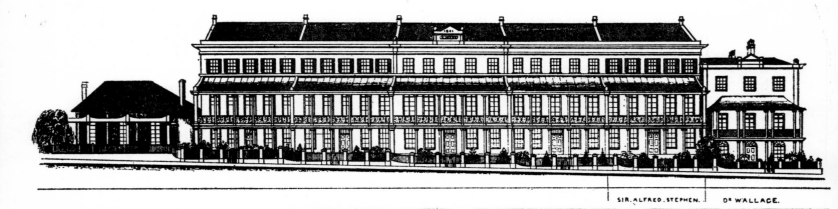

SIR.ALFRED.STEPHEN. | DR WALLACE.

Figure 12   Lyon's Terrace, Hyde Park, built in 1841, shows the original Sydney terrace type with roofed balconies and verandas, before the introduction of solid external party walls (as in pl. 359). The partitions were later made compulsory as a safety measure. The architecture here is still basically of late Georgian type (compare pl. 351). (From Sydney in 1848, *by Joseph Fowles)*

Figure 12

Plate 366

Plates 352, 354, 358, 363, 367, 377, 378

Plate 359

Plate 367

nearer suburbs, the primitive colonial vernacular had almost disappeared, to be replaced by Georgian, Gothic, Tudor Revival and Italianate forms. Baronial styles and Victorian exuberance produced combinations which could well be grouped under the term Picturesque. The mode of usage of cast iron, typically with filigree columns, fits in well either in detached houses of varying design or in terraces. Areas often considered by authorities to be worthy only of destruction may be the most picturesque, and capable of restoration to surprising attractiveness.

The hilly nature of the terrain adds to the vistas, and the varying architectural solutions to the problem give added interest to the houses and their ironwork. Many houses were constructed to give views of the harbour and to catch the cooling evening breezes. Even narrow terrace houses have surprising internal space and their stereotyped arrangement is such as to provide quiet privacy. Alas, the motorcar has reduced the peace and high-rise buildings have obliterated views of the harbour. Nevertheless, Sydney remains one of the world's most interesting cities.

Different areas of the capital of New South Wales present such sociological and topographical variations that it is reasonable to look at the city by neighbourhoods.

Plates 351, 352

Miller's Point and The Rocks, being situated between Sydney Cove and the neighbouring maritime region to the west, developed early and rapidly, and acquired an unsavoury reputation from the sailors released after long voyages. Early streets, clustered around the dock area, show primitive copies of English houses which were to become transmuted into the Sydney type. The area was recorded in photographs by Norman Selfe (1839–1911), civil engineer and chief draughtsman to the iron founders P. N. Russell and Co.

Plates 354, 355

Skirting the Royal Botanic Gardens and crossing The Domain one may enter Woolloomooloo, a previously fascinating area matching its unusual name. However, slum-like conditions and its nearness to the centre of Sydney tragically led to its destruction before civic consciousness was sufficiently aroused.

66

Plates 356–358

The district of Glebe originated in the church land for which provision had been made in 1789, in instructions from London to Arthur Phillip, 'Captain-General and Governor-in-Chief' of New South Wales:

> And it is Our further Will and Pleasure that a particular spot in or as near each town as possible be set apart for the building of a church, and four hundred acres adjacent thereto allotted for the maintenance of a minister, and two hundred for a school-master.

The development of the area is definitively described by Bernard and Kate Smith in *The Architectural Character of Glebe, Sydney* (1973). The land was first used for farming by the Rev. Richard Johnson, first chaplain to the new colony, who stigmatized it as '400 acres for which I would not give 400 pence'. However, it remained the property of the Church of England, and after subdivisions over a number of years it came to hold a cross-section of the community. The changes of level as Glebe falls away towards the water produce some fascinating profiles in streets of terrace houses, and the district also has a number of large detached houses, some of which have unusual arrangements of cast iron ornamentation.

Plate 356
Plates 359, 360

Paddington, in contrast to Woolloomooloo, has undergone preservation and restoration due to the citizens of the area banding together into the Paddington Preservation Society, which developed an enormous potential of energy. The realization that the units form splendid town houses for those working in the city, with amazing privacy and historical value, probably began the movement. Paddington consists largely of simple terrace houses on small frontages, built for workers in the city.

Plates 361–364

The best approach to Hunter's Hill is by ferry. The greater peace of the waterways sets a proper mood for the peacefulness of this region, about four miles from Sydney as the crow flies. Standing on a promontory between the Parramatta and Lane Cove Rivers as they run to enter Port Jackson, it remained relatively undisturbed for many years until it was marred by a freeway. In many ways it has retained an English character, with its lanes and hedges and magnificent old trees. Some of the stone houses are in an excellent state of preservation, and a feature of the area is the finely built stone walls.

Plate 364

Much of the architecture was due to the creativeness of the Joubert brothers, who settled there in 1840. Many skilled Italian artisans worked on the houses, and some materials were specially imported from France and Italy. One of the loveliest houses, St Malo, was demolished in 1961 to make way for the freeway.

Plate 362

Set in beautiful grounds overlooking Lane Cove, the house was built by Didier Numa Joubert in 1847. The ground on which it was built originally belonged to Mrs Reiby, who as a fourteen-year-old child in England caught and rode a neighbour's pony. For this she was arrested and sentenced to transportation for life. She was assigned as nursemaid at Government House, married the mate of the ship in which she was transported, and emerged as a rich business woman of high standing in the colony.

Melbourne, Victoria

Plates 381–416

Architecturally, early Melbourne and its ring of inner suburbs is a Victorian city. Founded in 1835 by two Tasmanian residents, Batman and Fawkner, seeking new fields for unimpeded endeavour, it remained a small town, little more than the centre of a pastoral settlement, expanding slowly by immigration, until in 1851 gold was discovered in Victoria and a gold rush began, not only within Australia, but also from other countries in spite of the long and arduous sea voyage. In 1851 the population of the colony was 77,340. Gold seekers brought the population to 231,925 in 1854, and in 1857 it had reached 410,766. The number of houses increased eightfold. As the available gold in the colony was exhausted, many disappointed miners left the capital city, but many remained, living in huts and tents. Those merchants who had profited from the gold rush demanded houses commensurate with their importance and wealth, and workmen wanted humbler dwellings to suit their means. Thus a building boom occurred between 1860 and 1890. At this time Victorian architecture from the homeland, with the inevitable time-lag occasioned by distance, gained ascendancy over the earlier Georgian styles of New South Wales and Tasmania. However, in many houses relative symmetry prevailed, although mouldings and doorways were becoming coarser and stucco decoration more pretentious.

Plates 396, 401
Plates 386, 398, 403, 405

Cast iron provided a means of adding decoration at a relatively small cost to single-storey houses, while it blossomed forth into a decorative 'apron', often ornate, always pleasing, on two-storey houses. The veranda and balcony served very useful functions, sheltering the door from rain and the windows from the hot summer's sun. The balcony in particular provided useful outdoor living space to

Plate 389

be enjoyed when the weather was temperate, and in the cool of a summer's evening. It is this façade which constitutes Melbourne's architectural distinction. Composed of balustrades, friezes, fringes, brackets and columns, the style was capable of great variation, and close inspection of the patterns adds interest to a walk in the city and its neighbouring suburbs. In early houses a cast iron fence fronted the veranda, and abutted on the pavement. A later ordinance compelled

Plates 393, 395, 396, 398

separation, so that a narrow garden strip intervened. Hollow square gate piers of cast iron are typical, especially a pattern with a lion's head in the centre of the pier and a round finial at the top. Complete aprons of iron are very common – a veranda on a single-storey house, a veranda and balcony on a two-storey house. The component parts are balustrades, columns with capitals, friezes and brackets. Sometimes a fringe is added below frieze and bracket, while spandrels (narrow castings) may link columns arranged in pairs or groups. The ironwork often achieved a delicate lace-like quality which removed it aesthetically from the drawing-rooms of the period, cluttered with a profusion of bric-a-brac and rather heavy furniture. Complete aprons are less frequent in other Australian cities.

Wood and later a very hard basalt ('blue-stone') were the usual early building materials. Later brick, usually covered with stucco, became dominant. Detached houses, pairs and terrace houses all have plain basic façades with often exuberant stucco decoration.

The financial collapse of 1890 brought this golden era of building to an abrupt end, and when building again gained momentum in Melbourne in Edwardian times, cast iron was regarded as old fashioned and was used no more.

NATIONAL TRUST HOUSES
Cast iron, fortuitously and fortunately, adorns three of the houses owned in Melbourne by the National Trust of Australia (Victoria).

Plates 381, 382

Pride of place goes to Como, the headquarters of the Trust. The house, of plain Georgian symmetry, was built in the mid 1850s before the building boom. In December 1864 it was bought by Charles Henry Armytage, a member of a pioneer pastoral family, and to cater for social life an east wing containing a ballroom was added in 1874. The property, of reducing acreage, remained in the hands of the Armytage family until 1959, when it was acquired by the Trust, aided by the generosity of the previous owners, the Misses Armytage.

Plate 384

In 1974, as the result of a legacy from the late Mrs Louisa Jones, the Trust was presented with Rippon Lea, a magnificent property including a mansion in the most beautiful private garden in Melbourne, some thirteen acres in extent. The house was begun in the late 1860s by F. T. Sargood, wholesale merchant, employing Joseph Reed and Frederick Barnes as architects. Its style is Italian Romanesque, with round arches of polychrome brick resting on colonnettes, and polished stone columns forming a loggia at the entrance. A cast iron *porte-cochère* was added during extensions in the 1880s.

In the garden next to the house is a huge lofty fernery with a cast iron frame, through which runs a creek on its way to the extensive lake. Narrows in the lake system are crossed by rustic bridges with cast iron railings. Alongside a swimming pool are two large urns of the same pattern as those in the garden of Corio Villa, which are illustrated in the catalogue of Charles D. Young of Edinburgh.

Plates 383, 385

Illawarra was begun to the design of James Birtwistle in 1889, a year after a land boom had reached its peak. It was built for Charles Henry James, one of the flamboyant figures in the most spectacular period of Victoria's commercial history. Reputed to be a millionaire, he was elected to the Legislative Council in 1887. The house was built to match his life style and as a symbol of his financial success. But in the two years when the house was being built the land boom collapsed into the depression of the early 1890s: the number of rooms was reduced and stucco trim replaced the freestone which had been originally intended. James lost his fortune and was twice declared insolvent, but the Illawarra estate had previously been transferred to his wife. Illawarra has unique interest as an example of the late period of cast iron ornamentation on a graceless exterior, brought into being by a flamboyant conjurer producing a reflection of his blatant personality. Illawarra's final private owner, Mr W. L. Ryan, generously presented the house to the Trust. There could be no better representative of the ostentation of the boom period.

Adelaide, South Australia

Plates 417–437

Adelaide, founded in 1836, may well claim to be the best-planned state capital in Australia, its present form being determined by a plan prepared by Colonel Light, Surveyor-General. The city, named at the request of King William IV in honour of his Queen, was divided into North and South Adelaide. The two parts were separated by a band of open country, about half a mile in breadth, through which flowed the Torrens River. The whole was surrounded by a broad green belt.

South Adelaide, now usually referred to simply as Adelaide, was planned on level ground south of the Torrens, approximately one square mile in extent, bounded by broad roadways named North, South, East and West Terraces. In

Plates 418–421

Plate 417

Plates 421, 424

Plates 419, 429

Figure 13

Plates 336, 337, 433, Figure 14

Plate 335

Figure 4

Plates 431–436

Plates 447, 448

Adelaide the word terrace implies an important roadway. The area contained by the four terraces has five squares, the central one being called Victoria Square. The rest was subdivided geometrically in grid fashion. This area became the commercial part of the city. North Adelaide arose from the river flats and parkland on the north side of the Torrens, and has remained largely residential.

Thus the city developed during the cast iron era, and fortunately much of the rich iron ornamentation remains, some even within the boundaries of the four terraces. As elsewhere in Australia, hotels have been particularly good preservers, and remarkable examples survive, notably at several intersections of the terraces, the corners of the original South Adelaide. In the business district balconies tend to rest on columns set out at the edge of the pavement, forming covered footpaths as in New Orleans. Upper balconies are often recessed, creating a tiered pyramidal effect. This recession increases sunny areas on the balcony, and allows more light to enter the windows. Long two-storeyed ornamented terraces of the type so common in Melbourne are rare in Adelaide. Where terraces occur, the divisions between houses are not solid as in Melbourne and Sydney, and party walls are not apparent on the façade. Pediments are a characteristic feature, on single houses or terraces. Yellow Mount Gambier stone is a common building material.

The ironwork itself is unusually well documented, thanks to the survival of fine catalogues of Adelaide foundries. For this reason the provenance of castings has been fully documented in the captions. G. E. Fulton conducted a foundry in the city for many years, but unfortunately little is known of the history of the firm. It published at least two catalogues. No copy of the first edition has been found, but the second edition of 1887 is a splendid catalogue, and its preface states that its size is more than double that of the first edition. Fulton died in July 1895.

Two editions of the catalogue of the 'Sun' Foundry were published, the first in 1897 and the second in 1914. The firm was founded by Colin Stewart, who had served his apprenticeship in the Sun Foundry in Scotland (see p. 24), and Allan Cameron Harley. The partnership was dissolved in 1910 and the business continued as A. C. Harley & Co. until about 1924, when Harley was bought out by Forwood, Down & Co.

The Harley catalogues appear to follow Fulton's, suggesting a direct continuity or the buying out of Fulton by Stewart and Harley. No direct evidence exists; but at a later stage the 'Sun' Foundry was using the floor and boxes of the old Fulton Foundry to produce castings.

Almost all the patterns illustrated are to be found in the catalogues. Relatively few patterns were registered in South Australia. Some patterns in the Adelaide catalogues were registered in other states for copyright purposes, and certainly copying existed, if only after copyrights expired. As we have seen (p. 52), the date of registration is not an accurate indication of the date of manufacture.

An interesting puzzle emerged when we found the trademark of Walter Macfarlane & Co. of Glasgow (pp. 23–24) on some castings in Adelaide, while the same patterns more frequently showed no name, or that of Fulton or Harley. Macfarlane's catalogue stated that its trademark was on all its products. Macfarlane may have had an agency in Adelaide, but whether the firms copied the pattern by agreement, purchase, or without the formality of either remains unknown. Other unmarked Macfarlane patterns are found in Brisbane.

Figure 13   Gates and fences from the 2nd edition of the catalogue of G. E. Fulton & Co. of Adelaide, 1887. No. 32 was registered in 1883 (pl. 335, no. 36).

No. 32.

No. 25.

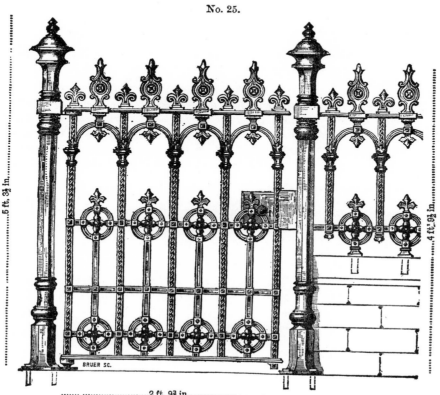

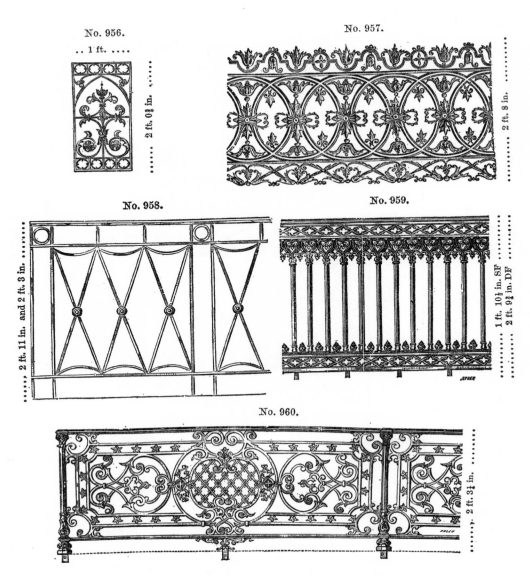

No. 956.

No. 957.

No. 958.

No. 959.

No. 960.

Figure 14   Balustrade patterns, from the 2nd edition of the catalogue of the 'Sun' Foundry (A. C. Harley & Co.), Adelaide, 1914. No. 957, based on circles and stylized acanthus leaves, was registered in Victoria in 1872 by Cross & Laughton; for a single-faced casting of this pattern in Sydney (upside-down), see pl. 358. No. 960, French in character, also appears in the catalogue of Macfarlane's of Glasgow, and a shorter version will be seen in Adelaide (pl. 434).

Brisbane, Queensland

Plates 438–455

Brisbane was named in honour of the Governor of New South Wales, Sir Thomas Brisbane, who dispatched John Oxley on an expedition which led to the formation of the first settlement at Moreton Bay in 1824. Subsequently Governor Gipps sent surveyors to lay out a township and parcel out the country for occupation. He ordered that the 'streets should not be wider than those of London, wide enough for the metropolis of the world'. Domestic building in Brisbane started in 1842, after the first land sale. The number of buildings increased after the formation of the state of Queensland in 1859.

Brisbane is subtropical, lying south of the tropic of Capricorn. The winter is warm and dry, the summer hot and wet. Gardens have to be watered in winter and not in summer. It is a climate in which insects flourish in tropical luxuriance, while exotic flowers adorn the gardens.

The typical Brisbane house developed as an adaptation to these climatic conditions. It was built of wood and raised above the ground on high stumps made of trunks of trees. These were given wider caps of metal, like inverted saucers, which prevented the upward spread of white ants in the wood. The posts might have to be replaced eventually, but the house was saved from the ravages of the ants. The raised arrangement allowed breezes to blow underneath the floor so that the houses were cooler than those set flat on the ground. The area under the floor, sheltered from rain, was a useful playground for children. It provided a well-ventilated, dry storage area, and clothes might be dried there. In the country, farm implements and even stock could be accommodated under the house.

Plate 438

Based on the platform so provided, the living part of the house formed a symmetrical or asymmetrical core, usually only one storey high. A wide roofed veranda was constructed on the front and one or more sides of the core. It provided a living and play area, and screens of varying types protected the inner rooms from direct sunlight while increasing privacy. The whole veranda could be screened against insects, and balustrades and screens prevented children from falling over the edge. Wide French windows or deep sash windows gave access to the rooms inside, while communication between the latter was assured by wide double doors. The whole arrangement allowed a free circulation of air, and was designed to catch as much of the breezes as possible. For this reason the early houses were built on every hill and knoll around the city.

Plates 439, 440

When galvanized iron became available it was almost always used as roofing material, thus adding the final blow to any aesthetic pretentions to which the common house might aspire. It transmits heat readily and to overcome this the pitch of the roof was usually steep to provide a large airspace, and tan bark was sometimes used for insulation. Large screened ventilators provided a circulation of air between roof and ceiling. The columns and balusters of the verandas were initially made of wood. From about 1860, ornamental cast iron was used for balustrades for the verandas and entrance steps. It was also used for screening ventilators and for the decoration of a pediment-like structure above the entrance to the veranda. When it became fashionable, cast iron might be substituted for an earlier wooden balustrade. In later houses cast iron columns might be used, but wood continued as a favoured material as it was lighter and cheaper. Flat filigree columns were also used.

Plate 439

Plates 440, 443

Plates 443, 445
Plate 439

Thus a definite Queensland vernacular was established. Hotels favoured the use of cast iron aprons with sometimes a deep frieze which served to keep the interior cool, and yet did not obstruct the cooling evening breezes. The large official buildings, built in the latter part of the nineteenth century, were usually made of stone, with roomy loggias and balconies, the latter being provided with cast iron balustrades, thus making an interesting association between Renaissance architecture and cast iron ornamentation.

Plates 446–448

Plates 451, 452

Considering the size of the city, a relatively large number of designs were registered. A high proportion of these were made by three foundry proprietors, J. Crase (with a number of different partners), A. Overend and Harvey Sargeant.

Plates 447–449, 455

Plate 455

It will be noted that some balusters have details on the external surface only. This lessened the cost because the molten iron was run directly into channels made by depressing the pattern into the surface of the sand in the box (see p. 12). No upper 'box' was required. In some instances, apparently to use less iron and to lighten the castings, the casting was hollowed out on the internal surface. This probably means that an upper 'box' was necessary. 'Single-faced' castings are commoner in Queensland than in other states.

Tasmania

The British settlement of Van Diemen's Land began in 1803, during the reign of George III. The first dwellings were crude shelters, built of the most readily available materials and of the simplest design and construction, usually having a central doorway with a window on each side. They resembled a young child's drawing of a house, which, whether of one or two storeys, has the symmetry of a Georgian house. (Maybe this is why the Georgian style evokes a primordial satisfaction within us.) A simple front veranda was often added, and thus the Tasmanian vernacular, similar to that of the mainland, appeared.

Plates 456, 457

Plates 459–461

As the land became settled memories of homeland houses led to their reproduction in the new country. Georgian and Regency styles were common in England at the time. Porticos are the most striking evidence of this importation to Tasmania. The British influence probably stimulated the use of cast iron for ornamentation on verandas and balconies, whether the houses were of elaborated vernacular, Georgian or Victorian styles. It seems that little ornamental ironwork was made in Tasmania. Veranda posts are frequently of wood, thus saving the cost of transport of heavy iron columns from the mainland.

New Zealand

Abel Janszoon Tasman sighted New Zealand in 1642 and gave the country its name. Over a hundred years later Captain Cook in the *Endeavour* annexed the country for England, but British interest was not officially proclaimed until 1840. An Anglican settlement was later founded at Canterbury in the South Island, and in 1852 the mother-country granted self-government to the colony. Wellington

Plate 467

Plates 463–465

was established as the capital in 1864. The discovery of gold was followed by a great increase in population, and after gold was exhausted, many of the miners remained to expand pastoral and mining interests. Thus it is that the cities were being built up in the cast iron era. Christchurch in the South Island is more like a cathedral city in England than any other colonial city we have seen. The Avon River and its lush green banks must have brought nostalgic memories to the settlers, and the many cast iron bridges which were built later did not spoil the stream. Some of the vistas including early buildings suggested homeland university cities.

6 Empires and Influences

India: Bombay

It is to be expected that iron ornamentation would be little used in countries in which mining and processing of iron ore was not carried out. In India, however, the British raj and the wealth of the East India Company and some of the citizens caused a considerable import trade of castings.

The East India Company paved the way for British intervention. A dual system of native and British government having proved a failure, Warren Hastings assumed the governorship of Bengal in 1772 and the governor-generalship of India in 1774. In 1858 Queen Victoria assumed the government of India, and in 1877 she was proclaimed Empress of India. Britain was the dominant external influence in a land lacking an iron industry, hence during the cast iron era the British influence would be strong.

Plates 468, 478

In *European Architecture in India 1750–1850* (1968) Sven Nilsson noted the importation of cast iron products:

> The freight lists of Danish East Indiamen include quantities of bar iron, and in the *Calcutta Gazette* we can see many sales notices concerning consignments including iron, both in the form of semi-finished and finished products. Finally all those cast-iron elements which were so popular in Europe during the 19th century were to be imported into India, but in the beginning, iron was scarce. An iron bridge constructed by John Rennie, who also designed Waterloo Bridge, was sent out from England in 1815, but was not mounted before 1844, in Lucknow. The college in Serampore, which was commenced in 1819, was supplied with a cast-iron fence, fanlights and a large staircase, all made in Birmingham.

The outbreak of the recent war between India and Pakistan interrupted a search for cast iron ornamentation in India and only Bombay could be photographed. Originally a Portuguese colony, Bombay became a British possession in 1661. As the island-city expanded, many-storeyed buildings were constructed to hold as many people as possible. Tiers of balconies jut out over the footpaths. In the nineteenth century cast iron balconies became fashionable, and were often attached to existing buildings. Wide and spacious, they provide living space, give protection from sun and monsoon rains, and serve to insulate the interior of the building. The ironwork patterns are usually of great delicacy.

Plates 469–477

Plates 469–471

Fences are often made of cast iron panels set above a solid base, and several of the patterns are identical or similar to designs shown in the catalogue of Macfarlane's Saracen Foundry of Glasgow. Macfarlane's also exported complete iron structures: a bank in Madras and a 'durbar hall' included in *Illustrated Examples of Macfarlane's Architectural Ironwork* are designed in what passed in Britain for the 'Hindoo' style – a sort of Brighton Pavilion fairytale style that was in fact based on Islamic Indian architecture.

A set of gates outside the former residence of the tycoon Sir David Sassoon, built in 1880 (since 1913 the Masina Hospital), reproduce with minor variations the design of the great gates displayed by the Coalbrookdale Company at the 1851 Great Exhibition, and now in London's Hyde Park. A balustrade in the Bassein Fort repetitively displayed the crowned profile of Queen Victoria in medallions framed by foliage scrolls, but it has unfortunately been removed and lost. (A photograph was reproduced in *The Times* of London of 18 June 1966.)

South Africa: Cape Town

Although the Portuguese discovered and explored the coast of South Africa, it remained for the Dutch to recognize the importance of the Cape as a provisioning station on the way to the East and to colonize it. Cape Town was founded in 1652. Eventually in 1814 the colony was ceded by Holland to the British Crown, and soon a large number of British settlers mingled with the Boers and Kaffirs. Troubles and wars arose, but the British influence was dominant and spread over Cape Colony, and in 1910 the Union of South Africa was established.

Dutch houses were naturally common in the eighteenth and early part of the nineteenth century. A number of buildings with distinctive shaped gables fronting the street, and central *stoeps* with gracefully curved flights of steps leading to the front door, remain as a reminder of Dutch architecture.

The Dutch aspect of Cape Town began to disappear after the middle of the nineteenth century. With the spread of the city, such buildings were replaced by shops, hotels and dwellings with English characteristics. Georgian, Regency, Victorian and Edwardian styles can all be recognized. The fine public buildings date from after 1860 and often have Renaissance features. Hence the mode of usage of cast iron is similar to that in Australia, both being derived from Britain, and indeed certain patterns registered in Australia appear in Cape Town. Much of the cast iron ornamentation has disappeared. A fine small book of Désirée Picton-Seymour's watercolours and scraper-board drawings, with annotation by R. I. B. Webster, vividly portrays Cape Town as it was in 1952: they regret the destruction which had already occurred and prophetically forecast the unfortunate demolition which was to follow.

Bermuda

The Bermuda group of islands form a British Crown colony which became an important naval and coaling station in 1869. St George, on the island of that name, was founded in 1794 and remained the capital until the latter was removed to Hamilton on the main island. It seems reasonable to expect that a prosperous colony would import ironwork when it was fashionable at home. St John's Pembroke Church, whose simple Gothic form suggests a village church in England, has gates, communion rails and grave fences made of imported cast iron added in the nineteenth century, and a bandstand in the Hamilton public gardens bears the name of George Smith & Co. of Glasgow. Recently, local reproduction of castings has also flourished, exemplified by a restaurant called Hoppin' John's in Front street, with both name and decor calculated to attract tourists. The latter are now mainly from the United States, and a number of the patterns reproduced are original New Orleans designs.

Plate 484

Canada

The first desultory contacts of Europeans with the region of Canada occurred towards the end of the fifteenth century, and early in the seventeenth century French settlements were established in what is now Nova Scotia and Quebec. In the eighteenth century France and England struggled for the territory, and by the Peace of Paris in 1763 the whole of New France was ceded to Great Britain. A state of symbiosis rather than close synthesis has resulted. The French preserved their individuality and their language in the Dominion of Canada, particularly in Quebec and Montreal. This explains the admixture of French and English influences in architecture and, to a discernible extent, in the usage of cast iron.

The most striking cast iron construction in Toronto is the fence of Osgoode Hall, now the Law Courts of Upper Canada, which was cast by the St Lawrence Foundry and erected in 1860. In Quebec the Terrasse Dufferin, high above and overlooking the St Lawrence River, is outstanding: it is a wide board-walk with a balustrade punctuated at intervals by large pavilions, set against the backdrop of the Citadelle and the spectacular Château Frontenac Hotel. The Séminaire de Québec has an arrangement of three unusually tall superimposed tiers of iron-work. From it one may walk along the Grande-Allée Saint-Louis through the region of Sainte-Ursule, a neighbourhood of stone terrace houses where small balconies over the entrance doors alternate with roofed balconies above polygonal bay windows. In Montreal some buildings closely echo Parisian styles.

Plate 485

Plates 489, 490

Plate 487

Plate 488

Tahiti

Tahiti, the largest of the Society Islands in the Pacific Ocean, was claimed for France in 1768. In 1836 French Catholic missionaries attempted to open a mission, and finally in 1843 a convention was signed placing the islands under French protection.

The French influence thus predominated at a time when cast iron was being extensively used in France, but little was in fact used in Tahiti. The Palais de Justice has columns of cast iron framing balusters of wrought iron, and the steps, veranda and balcony of the Mission Catholique have a brave display of cast iron. The cemetery, as in many countries, has a number of cast iron railings and religious symbols. Open in design and light in weight, these could be imported relatively cheaply. Some are only single-faced, as we have already seen in Queensland. The letter-boxes on the island are of the standard French wall-mounted type, bearing the initials 'RF' for République Française, and were certainly cast in France.

Plate 491
Plate 492

Mauritius

The island of Mauritius in the Indian Ocean was discovered in 1505. After a period of Portuguese and Dutch control, it was held from 1715 to 1769 by agents of the French East India company, and used during the war between England and France as a base to harass English East Indiamen. The British were thus anxious to capture the island, and in the peace of 1814 British ownership was confirmed. However, it was agreed that the inhabitants should retain their own laws, customs and religion, and the island remains largely French. Ironwork patterns were discovered that relate to foundries in both Paris and Glasgow. The gates and railing of the Pamplemousses Botanical Gardens (*pamplemousse* means grapefruit) won a first prize in the Great Exhibition of 1851 in London; according to an obelisk in the main avenue of the gardens, they were the gift of a M. Lienard, whose name also appears elsewhere in Mauritius. There seems no doubt that Lienard was the Parisian sculptor in wood who worked with the iron founders Barbezat & Cie. and other French firms (see pl. 496, and, for examples of his sculpture, pp. 73–74 in *The Art-Journal Catalogue: The Industry of all Nations*, 1851, reprinted as *The Great Exhibition: London 1851* by David & Charles, Newton Abbot, 1970). Lienard's name is also seen at Launceston in Tasmania as the sculptor of a fountain cast at the foundry of Barbezat & Cie.

Plates 493, 494, 496
Plate 495

Mexico

Mexico City gained its most remarkable example of cast iron through imperial connections, but on the anniversary of its independence. The Kiosco de la Alameda de Santa Maria, an extraordinary Moorish pavilion constructed entirely of cast iron, is truly a portable building. It was made in Spain in 1889, to a design by the architect Ramón Ibarrola, and sent to the Paris International Exhibition of that year. Afterwards it was shipped to Mexico City as a gift from the Spanish government to commemorate Mexican independence. There it was initially placed in the central park, but in 1909 it was moved to another park, the Alameda de Santa Maria, where it has remained since.

Another unusual feature of the ironwork of Mexico City is a distinctive type of long ornamental public bench, cast locally. Balcony balustrades are relatively uncommon and show French influence, which was probably established by an iron firm trading with France rather than any closer national link. Several designs from the Parisian catalogue of Barbezat & Cie. were found.

Plates 497–501

Plate 497
Plates 502, 503

The Plates

1 Characteristics of wrought iron, as opposed to cast iron (see pp. 12–13): the central motif of the famous Sword Gate at Charleston, South Carolina, shows the basic thin strips of iron, hammered out and bent into curls; separate leaves of *repoussé* work (hammered from the back); and joins made by fusing the strips or fixing them with bands. (The strips of wire are of course not original.)

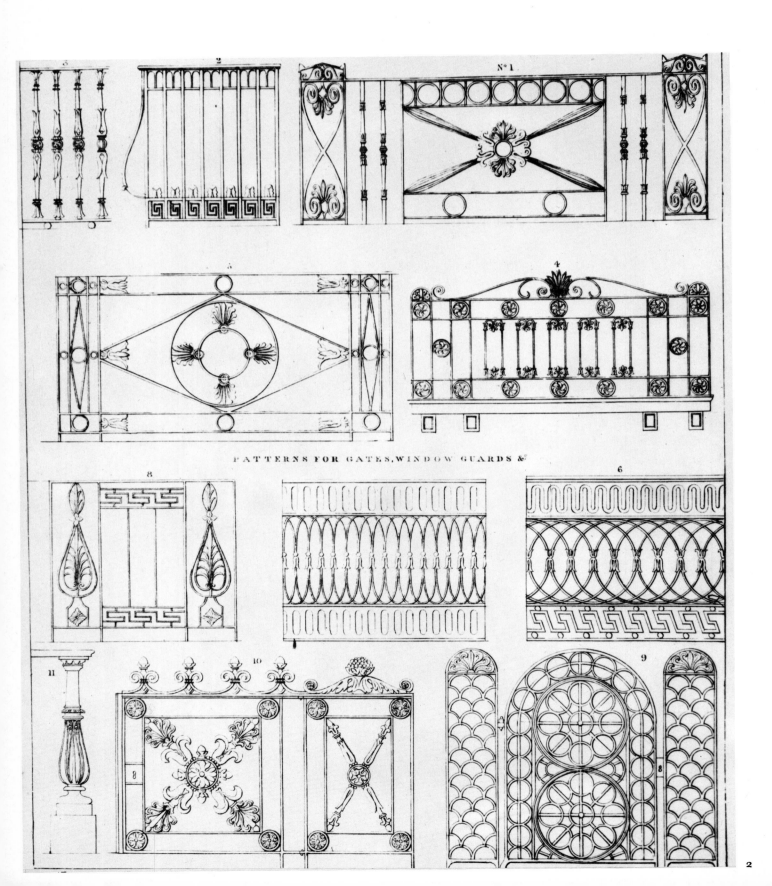

PATTERNS FOR GATES, WINDOW GUARDS &c.

Patterns for Window Guards and Balcony Railing executed in London

3

Plates from L. N. Cottingham's *The Smith and Founder's Director*, published in London in 1824 (see pp. 19–21). The book recorded existing designs as well as new patterns, and had an influence far beyond Britain.

2 'Patterns for Gates, Window Guards, &c.'. Pattern no. 1 at the top appears in the Regent's Park terraces (pl. 40) and in Tasmania (pl. 456), and a variant on no. 4 will be seen at Leamington (pl. 81).

3 'Patterns for Window Guards and Balcony Railing executed in London'. No. 7, combined with no. 4 in the plate opposite, will be seen at Leamington; the design bottom right, with anthemia below a wave motif, possibly designed by Robert Adam (see pl. 35), is one of the most common of all English balcony patterns (pls. 54, 71, 72, 74, 77) and was even exported to Sydney (pl. 351).

4

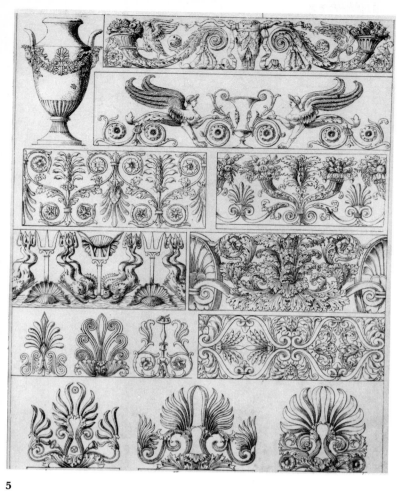

5 **6**

Plates from Cottingham's 1824 *Director*

4 'Roman Ornament for Borders, Pilasters, Friezes &c.'. Grapevines and acanthus leaves figure prominently, with birds and animals. The pattern in the centre with a leaping dog was copied in Philadelphia (pls. 263, 264). **5** 'Enrichments for Borders, Pannels &c., in the Grecian & Roman style': a skull decorated with ribands, cornucopia with fruit, mythical creatures on each side of an urn (compare Athens, pl. 197), dolphins, shells and Neptune's trident (compare Leningrad, pls. 133–135), acanthus leaves and variations on the anthemion.
6 A design for a covered balcony based on rosettes and Ionic volutes, with vases in the frieze and the caduceus of Mercury at the top.

7 A drawing by Cottingham of a stair with *rinceau* balustrade and candelabrum (authors' collection).

7

8

9

8 'Piers and Lamps for Gates, and Palisade Fences', from Cottingham's 1824 *Director*. The pattern on the left, without the lamp, was used in Regent's Park (pl. 39). 9 A drawing by Cottingham of a balustrade identical to the one used in Belgrave Square: see pl. 55 (authors' collection).

10 A plate from Henry Shaw's *Examples of Ornamental Metal Work*, published in London in 1836 (see p. 21): 'Railing, at the Entrance to Hyde Park, from Piccadilly'. The castings, based on anthemion and acanthus leaves and set between massive stone piers, are those of Decimus Burton's 1825 screen and railings by Apsley House.

RAILING,

at the Entrance to Hyde Park, from Piccadilly.

Scale   Feet.

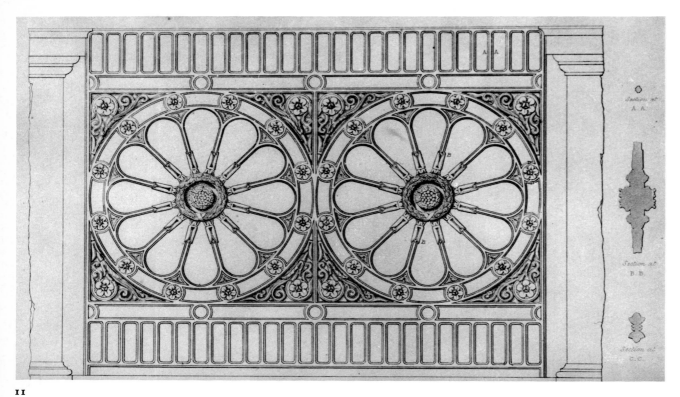

11

Illustrations from Shaw's *Examples of Ornamental Metal Work*, 1836 (see p. 21)

11 'Balcony Railing. From the United service Club-house, Waterloo Place'. From the predecessor of the present club, designed by Sir Robert Smirke in 1816. Shaw's illustration, dated 1825, shows the wheel motif that was one alternative to anthemion patterns in Neo-classical design (compare pl. 3).
12 'Balcony Railing, from Upper Woburn Place. The Railing Designed by H. Shaw. The Bracket by L. Vulliamy, Archt. Executed by Messrs. T. W. & L. Cubitt.' Several houses from this development in north Bloomsbury, built *c.* 1824–25, survive, with their ironwork, opposite the Neo-Greek St Pancras Church. For an echo in Cape Town, see pl. 479. **13** 'Staircase Railings'. All but 2 and 6 were designed by Shaw himself. No. 2 was in the Greek Revival house of the collector Thomas Hope; no. 6 was designed by W. and D. Bailey.

12

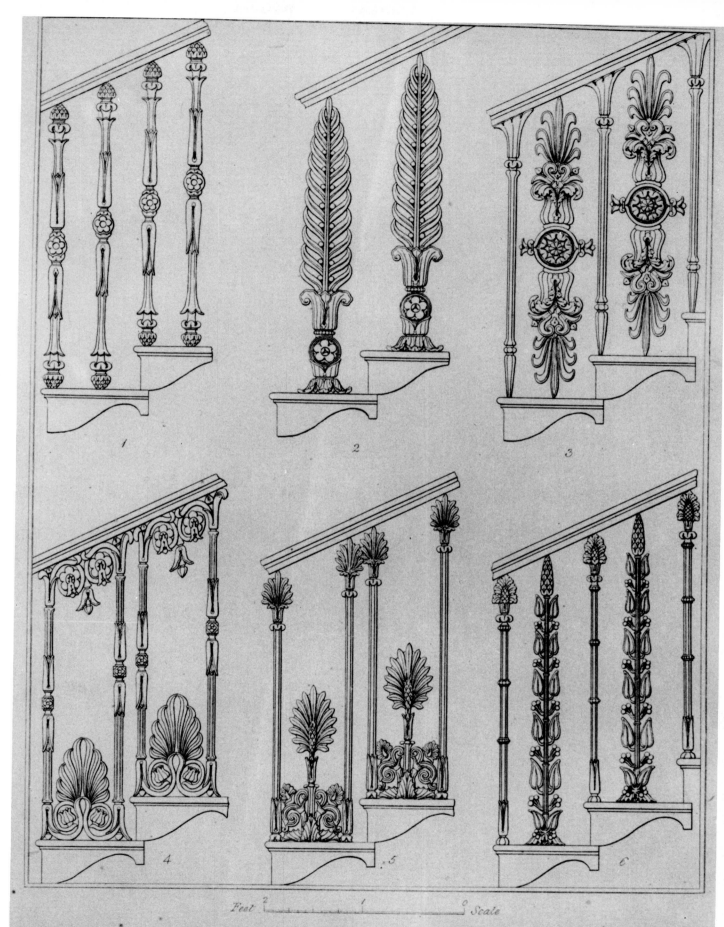

1   2   3

4   5   6

Feet [2   1   0] Scale

STAIRCASE RAILINGS.

Nº 2. From the Mansion of Thoˢ Hope Esqʳ. Nº 6. Desᵈ by W. & D. Bailey. Nº 1.3.4.5. Desᵈ by H. Shaw.

London, Pubᵈ May 1826, by Priestley & Weale, High Street, Holborn.

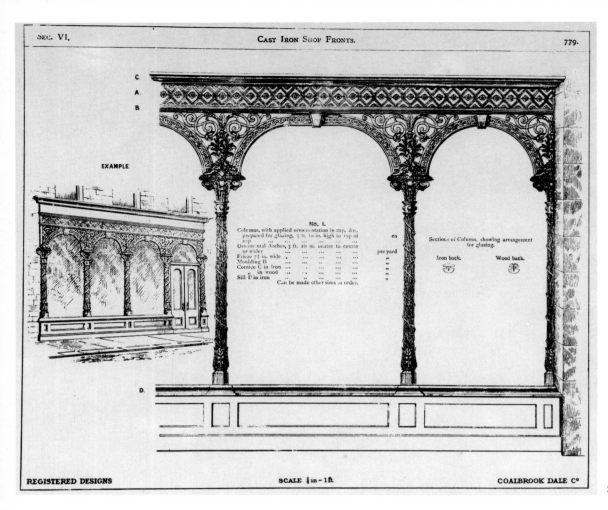

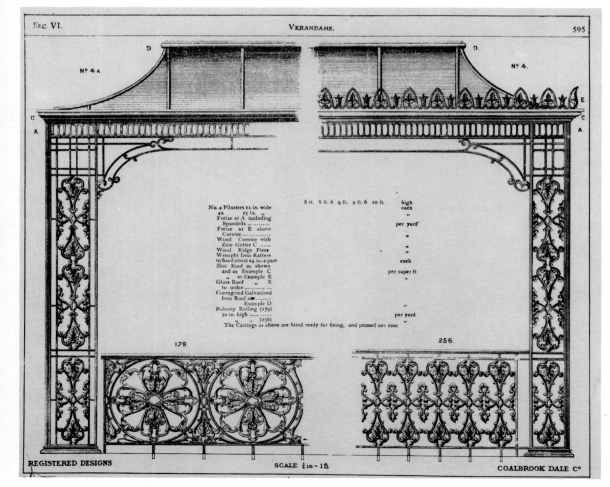

Illustrations from the Coalbrookdale Company's *Catalogue of Castings and Works in Metal*, 1875 (see pp. 21–22).

14 A cast iron shop front with large plate-glass windows (compare pls. 84, 85). **15** Two patterns for verandas or covered balconies. **16** Stair balusters. Classical allusions have almost entirely vanished (compare pl. 13). A design similar to no. 39A will be seen again (pls. 31, 379).

For wide Steps these patterns may be alternated by single Baluster.—See pages 564 to 566.

All Balusters are priced unfitted.   For Fitting see page 566.

60A
36 in. and under.

45A
39 in. and under.

39A
39 in. and under.

58A
36 in. and under

59A
in. and under.

REGISTERED DESIGNS   SCALE 1in = 1ft   COALBROOK DALE Cº

16

17 A finely cast balustrade by Newton, Chambers & Co., of the Thorncliffe Iron Works near Sheffield. Three different widths of the pattern are offered, with variations in detail, and the end post incorporates a pot for mignonettes. The diamond-shaped mark at the bottom shows that it was registered against copying on 12 April 1853 (see pp. 25–26).

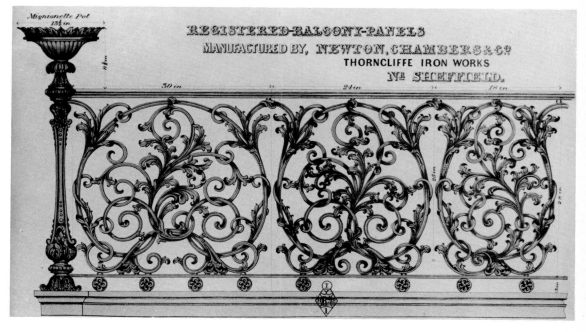

Mignonette Pot
13¼ in

REGISTERED BALCONY PANELS
MANUFACTURED BY NEWTON, CHAMBERS & Cº
THORNCLIFFE IRON WORKS
Nª SHEFFIELD.

30 in   24 in   18 in

17

18

Walter Macfarlane & Co., Saracen Foundry, Glasgow

18 The façade of the factory, showing many usages of cast iron, including lettering, two types of chimney-cap and a tower with dome and lantern. From the 5th edition of the catalogue, 1870/71. **19** Stair balusters registered on 3 June 1867, from the 5th edition of Macfarlane's catalogue. For the actual balustrade see p. 99. **20** Screen for a pleasure ground, registered on 28 April 1875, from Macfarlane's *Examples Book*. **21** A fantasy showing a range of ornamentation, from gate piers to roof cresting, registered on 5 March 1875, from the *Examples Book*.

19

20

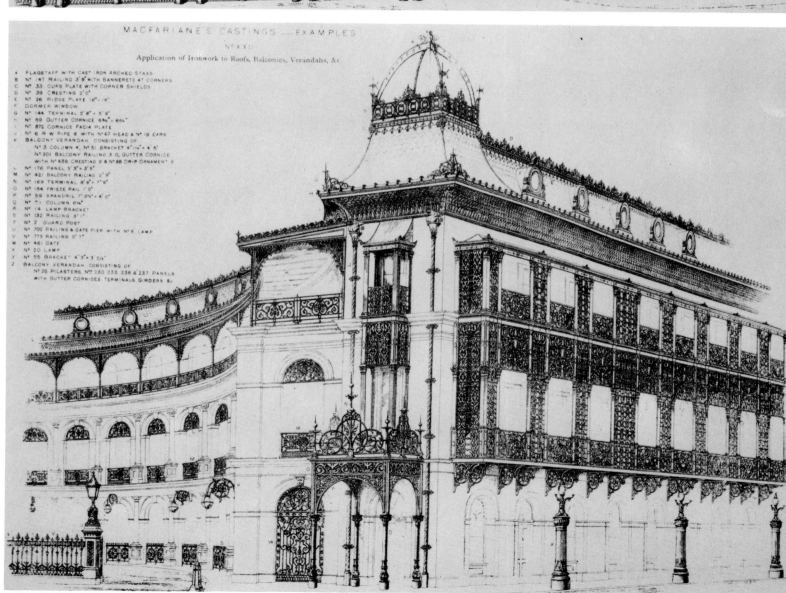

MACFARLANE'S CASTINGS — EXAMPLES

Nº XXII

Application of Ironwork to Roofs, Balconies, Verandahs, &c.

A   FLAGSTAFF WITH CAST IRON ARCHED STAYS
B   Nº 147 RAILING 3' 9" WITH BANNERETS AT CORNERS
C   Nº 33 CURB PLATE WITH CORNER SHIELDS
D   Nº 39 CRESTING 2' 0"
E   Nº 26 RIDGE PLATE 16"×16"
F   DORMER WINDOW
G   Nº 144 TERMINAL 2' 6" × 5' 9"
H   Nº 89 GUTTER CORNICE 6¾" × 6¼"
I   Nº 872 CORNICE FACIA PLATE
J   Nº 6 R W PIPE 6 WITH Nº 47 HEAD & Nº 19 EARS
K   BALCONY VERANDAH CONSISTING OF
    Nº 3 COLUMN 4, Nº 51 BRACKET 4' 1½" × 4' 5"
    Nº 201 BALCONY RAILING 3' 0, GUTTER CORNICE
    WITH Nº 439, CRESTING 9 & Nº 88 DRIP ORNAMENT 5
L   Nº 176 PANEL 5' 3" × 3' 5"
M   Nº 421 BALCONY RAILING 2' 9"
N   Nº 169 TERMINAL 8' 9" × 7' 9"
O   Nº 154 FRIEZE RAIL 1' 0"
P   Nº 59 SPANDRIL 7' 0½" × 4' 0"
Q   Nº 51 COLUMN 6¾"
R   Nº 14 LAMP BRACKET
S   Nº 132 RAILING 3' 1"
T   Nº 2 GUARD POST
U   Nº 702 RAILING & GATE PIER WITH Nº 5 LAMP
V   Nº 773 RAILING 5' 7"
W   Nº 461 GATE
X   Nº 20 LAMP
Y   Nº 55 BRACKET 4' 3" × 3' 2½"
Z   BALCONY VERANDAH CONSISTING OF
    Nº 26 PILASTERS, Nº 230 233 236 & 237 PANELS
    WITH GUTTER CORNICES TERMINALS GIRDERS &c

21

23

Walter Macfarlane & Co., Saracen Foundry, Glasgow

22 A shopping arcade, registered on 27 February 1875, from the *Examples Book*. **23** A balcony featuring anthemion and acanthus, from the 6th edition of the catalogue (1882–83). The design appears in Brisbane: see pls. 447 and 448. **24** A bandstand, from the 6th edition of the catalogue. One was exported to Adelaide (pls. 435, 436). **25** A 'Lamp Pillar', from the *Examples Book* (1876). **26** A fountain popular throughout Britain and the Empire (pl. 462): a large version of a type registered in 1860 (see p. 24), it was still current in 1911. From the 6th edition of the catalogue. **27** Gate piers of *c.* 1871. For their use in Adelaide, see pls. 431 and 432.

24

25

26

27

28

George Smith & Co., Sun Foundry, Glasgow

28 The façade of the factory, from their undated *Catalogue of Architectural and Ornamental Castings.* **29** Ornamental pavilion and clock tower erected at Bridgeton Cross, from the catalogue.

29

30

1' 4"

OPENING 4½" × 4½"

1' 7"

PROJECTS
10½"

30 Ornamental Gothic rainwater head made by the Milton Iron Works of McDowall, Steven & Co., Glasgow; from the 21st edition of their catalogue, *Architecture & General Iron Castings.*

Watson, Gow & Co., Etna Foundry, Glasgow (see pp. 24–25)

31, 32 Balusters, and components for verandas and balconies, from the catalogue. The railing no. 283 and veranda no. 194 were used in other countries, and can be seen in Australia, for instance, at Sydney and in Tasmania (see pls. 362 and 458, and compare pl. 154); balusters resembling no. 55 appear in Beirut (pl. 506).

31

32

33

London

33 The iron railings and gates of St Paul's Cathedral, cast in the Sussex Weald by Richard Jones and erected in 1714 (see p. 16). **34** Gates in the railings of St Martin-in-the-Fields, 1726, designed, like the church, by James Gibbs.

35

London

35, 36 No. 7 Adam Street, a surviving fragment of the Adelphi scheme begun by Robert and James Adam in 1768 (see p. 17). The stucco ornamentation of the pilasters echoes the anthemion design of the first floor balconettes and the window guards higher up. The latter appear in Cottingham's 1824 *Director* (pl. 3), and were an extremely popular pattern. They and the balconettes may have been designed by Robert Adam and cast by the Carron Company (see pp. 17, 22).

37

38

39

London

The Regent's Park development (see p. 26)

37 A lyre pattern on Ulster Place, *c.* 1824, at the corner of Park Square West. **38** Massive hollow gate piers at No. 40 St Andrew's Place, near Park Square East, built by Nash in 1823–25. Such posts are uncommon in London. **39** Taller panels punctuate the garden fences in Nash's Park Crescent, of 1812–22. The railing of spears and anthemion pier are illustrated by Cottingham, but he shows the pier ending in a lamp (pl. 8). **40** One of the end pavilions of Hanover Terrace, built by Nash in 1822–23. The balustrade panels here and at Cornwall Terrace nearby are slight modifications of those in Cottingham's 1824 *Director* (see pl. 2, no. 1).

40

41

44

42

43

London balconies

41 A common early pattern, Gothic in inspiration, seen here in Montague Street, Bloomsbury, built by James Burton in 1800. We shall see this design again, as far away as Sydney in Australia (pls. 72, 107, 351).
42 Again in Bloomsbury, wide panels of simple pattern are relieved by narrow Neo-classical insets, most of which have disappeared. The delicate glazing bars of the Georgian fanlight appear widened by paint.
43 A light curvaceous design with acanthus as the central motif alternating with spiral-twisted bars, on No. 47 Bryanston Square, Marble Arch. The balcony is later in date than the house, built in 1811.
44 Complexity increases as castings of three different widths use decorative motifs varying from irregular diamonds to parrots on perches. **45-47** Contrasts in 19th-century designs: weapons united by a wreath, a massive *rinceau* design, and a busy yet satisfying pattern of castings, round in section. The latter two probably date from the 1840s.

45

46

47

48

London

Uses of cast iron

48 A roofed balcony at No. 12 Bedford Square, Bloomsbury, adds elaboration to the plain Georgian façade built *c.* 1775. The elements are rosettes and acanthus, with lattice infil and a solid fringe of wave pattern (possibly wood, since removed) at the top. The fine fanlight is made of cast iron, and the decorations around the door are also mould-made, in Coade stone, a patented composition. **49** A rare arrangement of roofed balconies above verandas. No. 56 Holland Park Avenue has filigree columns with brackets and frieze, while its neighbour has thin round columns. **50** An unusual cast iron portico at No. 21 Upper Berkeley Street, W.1, is capped by an open balcony. The design appears in the 6th edition of the catalogue of Macfarlane's of Glasgow, 1882–83. **51** In Chepstow Road, Notting Hill, a semi-basement is surmounted by a roofed veranda, which, in turn, forms the floor of an open balcony.

50

51

London

The Thurloe Estate, South Kensington (see p. 26)

52 Thurloe Square, built under the direction of George Basevi in 1843. In its ironwork classical forms are being abandoned in favour of a daintier effect. The projecting porches provide a new position for ornament (see pl. 55). **53** Egerton Crescent, probably also by Basevi, has different castings, now frankly Rococo in inspiration, while stucco covers the brickwork and Ionic capitals replace Doric. **54** Alexander Place was extended in 1839, again probably by Basevi, and named in honour of the landowner John Alexander. The balconies have the familiar anthemion pattern (pls. 3, 35).

London

55 A balcony over a porch in Belgrave Square, designed in the 1820s by Basevi and built by Cubitt's. The anthemion and rosette pattern was drawn by Cottingham (pl. 9). **56** A variation on the same theme, at No. 41 Southwick Place, Bayswater, *c.* 1840. Curved balustrades were more complicated to make and hence more expensive than flat ones. Here pineapples on urns complete the composition. **57** Pairs of curved balconettes rise in steps on relatively modest two-bay houses, built in the 1830s (and now demolished) in Ampton Street, W.C.1. **58, 59** Exuberant Victorian eclecticism at the corner of Queen's Gate and Queen's Gate Place, Kensington, designed *c.* 1860 by C. J. Richardson. In the ironwork, faintly classical balusters (compare pls. 12, 13) are entangled in garlands and foliage trails.

56

57

58

59

61

60

62

London

60, 61 Gates between Hyde Park and Kensington Gardens, cast by the Coalbrookdale Company and shown at the Great Exhibition of 1851. For the same pattern exported to Bombay, see pl. 475. **62, 63** The Smithfield Meat Market, built in 1866–67 by the City Architect, Sir Horace Jones: a functional building cheered by richly decorative cast iron.

63

64

London

64, 65 A lost monument of cast iron: the Coal Exchange, designed by J. B. Bunning and built in 1846–49 (see p. 27). A contemporary illustration shows its original appearance, with large paintings of fossil ferns around the base of the iron-and-glass dome. The iron-floored galleries, off which offices opened in three tiers, and the structural members patterned with cables – the balustrades even seeming to be made of looped ropes – are seen in a photograph taken shortly before the building's tragic and unnecessary demolition in 1962.

66

Brighton

66-69 Madeira Drive, 1888–95. The structural columns double as drainpipes, and at the base of each a dolphin's mouth discharges rainwater. The lattice pattern of the arches, inspired by the Royal Pavilion, is further embellished by alternating male and female heads set as keystones at the top (pl. 69).

70 A staircase in the Royal Pavilion, remodelled by Nash in 1815–22. It is of iron cast and painted to simulate bamboo, with exotic serpents at the ends of the treads.

67

68

69

70

71

72

Brighton

71, 72 The bows and balconies of Regency Square, begun in 1818. The two patterns seen on the left in pl. 72 are among the most common in southern England (see the note on pl. 3, and pl. 41), and were even exported to Sydney (pl. 351). The massive iron brackets in pl. 71 are similar to those illustrated by Henry Shaw (pl. 12). 73 The Grand Hotel, built in 1862–64 by J. Whichcord, has six layers of balconies running the full length of the façade in the Parisian manner, here justified by the hotel's position facing the sea.

73

Cheltenham

74 No. 20 Priory Parade, after 1830. A balcony of great delicacy with curvaceous wrought iron scrolls and filigree columns. The balustrade is of the common anthemion pattern (see pls. 71, 72, opposite), with alternating narrow panels (compare pl. 77). **75** Massive castings of anthemion and palmette at No. 5 Columbia Place, Winchcombe Street, of *c.* 1820–25. The absence of an upper railing is unusual, but similar designs occur in London. **76** No. 36 Oxford Parade. Castings in a frame of wrought iron, with a fringe of cast iron on the balcony and the canopies above the windows, give an unusual appearance. The ironwork was added after 1845 to a house of *c.* 1820.

75

76

77

78

Leamington Spa

77–80 Clarendon Square, begun *c.* 1825. An entrance is guarded by a cast iron griffin. In pl. 77 the balcony again has the common anthemion pattern; narrow castings, embodying the anthemion design, form the bases of openwork columns filled with overlapping circles. They appear in conjunction with the same balustrade, but the other way up, at Cheltenham (pl. 74). The bent-ribbon patterns in pl. 78 are unusual, except for the band of Greek key running along the top. In pls. 79 and 80, the same elements based on the anthemion serve for a covered balcony on one house and a basement fence nearby. The design is an elaboration of one illustrated by Shaw (pl. 12). In pl. 80 the anthemion design is ingeniously expanded on the gate, while in pl. 79 the narrow baluster with circular centre and anthemia at either end is repeated vertically for the columns. **81** A light balustrade in Lansdowne Crescent, *c.* 1840, combines two patterns in Cottingham (pl. 2, no. 4 and pl. 3, no. 7). The wide columns embody the Greek key pattern.

79

80

81

82

83

Great Malvern

82 A chestnut capital in the railway station of 1860–61, designed by E. W. Elmslie.
83 The geometrical ironwork of the Foley Arms Hotel, built in 1810 (wings were added in 1812 and 1817). The lettering above the veranda is also of cast iron.

84, 85 A Victorian iron shop front in a country town in the south of England, representative of many that have disappeared, parallels an illustration in the *Examples Book* of Macfarlane's Saracen Foundry in Glasgow (see p. 24). The number of windows – making the most of plate glass – has increased, and the whole shop front projects; but only the ventilator grille and column bases are significantly different. The shop design was registered in 1875, Macfarlane's iron 'Sign Alphabet' in 1862.

DRAPERS & SILK MERCERS

85

84

SCATS

86

87

Edinburgh

86 A doorway in Charlotte Square, designed by
Robert Adam in 1791. The decorative ironwork
comprises area railings (as usual modelled on
spears), lamp holder with cone-shaped snuffer and
fanlight. **87** A three-bay balcony at No. 58 Great
King Street, built before 1823. The pattern is shown
in the catalogue of the Sun Foundry of Glasgow (see
p. 24; sect. II, pl. 106, no. 410). **88** Balconettes next
door in Great King Street, slightly Rococo in
character. As often in Edinburgh, the windows have
lost their Georgian glazing bars. **89** The fanlights of
Edinburgh have a delightful lightness of design,
similar to those of London and Dublin (pls. 42, 48,
114). Many such patterns appear in J. Bottomley's
Book of Designs, published in 1793. **90** A first-floor
balconette at No. 32 India Street, of the type also
used nearby in the Royal Circus of 1820–23. **91** A
wide balcony at No. 12 India Street. The bands of
which the design is composed are grooved, giving a
richer effect than plain bars.

88

89

90

91

92

93

94

Edinburgh

92, 95 The balcony railing of No. 13 Manor Place, with its anthemion pattern above palmettes, its swirling acanthus leaves and ribbon swags, seen from below and from a window. A grid flooring, increasing the amount of light reaching ground floor windows, is usual in Edinburgh. The anthemion design of the picket heads on the area railing below echoes the balcony.
93 No. 47 Melville Street, of the 1820s. On the lamp holders snakes' heads act as torch extinguishers (compare pl. 86). The railing spikes have an elegant openwork design, and pineapple finials adorn the posts of the gate which gives access to the basement.

The Earl of Moray's estate, laid out in 1822 by James Gillespie Graham

94 The ironwork on Nos. 6 and 7 St Colme Street has a geometrical design, bounded by a Greek key pattern. **96, 97** Moray Place, designed on a grand scale as individual houses. The balconettes (pl. 96 shows that of No. 23 Moray Place) have a bold anthemion design that was widely used in Edinburgh and Glasgow (pl. 104).

95

96

97

98

99

100

Edinburgh

98 A detail of the gates of Fettes College, designed by David Bryce, incorporating the school's coat of arms and happily providing the date 1874. **99** The staircase of No. 34 Buckingham Terrace. The baluster pattern is recorded in the catalogues of Macfarlane's Saracen Foundry of Glasgow, with the registration date 3 June 1867 (pl. 19). **100** The Royal Scottish Museum, with an internal skeleton of cast iron incorporating simple balustrades, designed by Captain Fowke of the Royal Engineers in 1861.

Glasgow

101 The common arrangement of area and entrance railings in the city (see also pl. 103). The castings – here based on palmettes below, and a fanciful anthemion above – are heavy, and the traditional row of spears (pl. 86) is forgotten. This pattern in Park Circus Place, designed by Charles Wilson in 1855–56, is shown in both the Macfarlane and Sun Foundry catalogues (see above, pp. 23–24).

Glasgow

102 Detail of a balustrade in Woodside Terrace, in which S-shaped scrolls are alternatively up-ended. **103** Area and entrance railings of the usual Glasgow type in Lynedoch Terrace. **104-106** Newton Place, designed by the Edinburgh architect George Smith in 1840. The balconettes on the central range of the terrace (pl. 104) have the attractive anthemion design common in Edinburgh (pl. 96), with the addition of corner posts. The long balconies of the end pavilions (pl. 105) have an anthemion design that appears in the catalogue of the Sun Foundry of Glasgow (see p. 24).

104

105

106

Dublin

Merrion Square North,
by John and George Ensor, 1762–64

107 Starting at the western end, one finds a
wonderful array of balconies, in which a number of
features uncommon in London are apparent. In the
foreground tall urns cap the four-sided posts of an
otherwise plain railing. Cast iron brackets support
the balconies which commonly have slatted iron
floors. Nos. 4 and 6 have covered balconies from
which the roof has been removed, a frequent
practice in Dublin allowing more light into the
house. The balustrade of No. 4 has a common early
'Gothic' pattern (see pl. 41) and anthemion
brackets, while No. 6 (see also pl. 109) is a later,
heavier design, with a crest, narrow frieze, fringe
and brackets. **108** The balcony of the corner house,
No. 1 (far left in pl. 107), has a pattern of
symmetrical scrolls. **109** A detail of the covered
balcony of No. 6: the roof supports have the same
pattern as the balustrade, framed between narrow
columns. Another Victorian balcony is visible at the
far right (see pl. 113).

110

Dublin

Merrion Square North

110-113 In Nos. 7–9 Victorian and Regency ironwork meet. The balustrade of No. 9 (pl. 112) is based on the anthemion, the filigree columns on a classical *rinceau*. The double-ended pattern at the base of the columns occurs in London (pl. 12), and as far away as Cape Town (pl. 479). The balcony of No. 8 (pl. 113, right) is a curious mixture: panels of 'Renaissance' pattern are topped by Gothic finials and rest on Regency consoles (compare pl. 12). No. 7 (on the left in pl. 113) recalls a pattern by Macfarlane's of Glasgow, and has in addition a fringe at floor level. Strong four-sided open posts, such as the one at No. 9 (pl. 111), are characteristic of Merrion Square; the railings here are of particularly elaborate design.

111   113

112

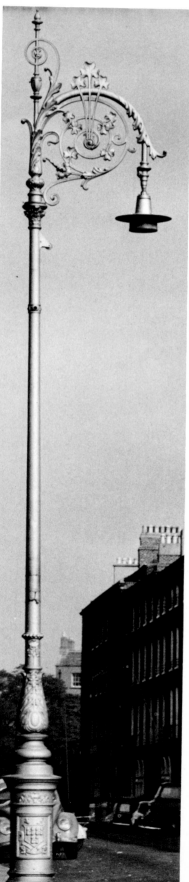

11[

Dublin

114 No. 41 Merrion Square South; the balcony is of somewhat heavy design with a fringe of anthemia below, whereas the doorway, incorporating a lantern, makes full use of delicate Adam motifs. **115** The Turf Club, at No. 25 Merrion Square North, proclaims its concern on its balconies. **116** A lamp standard in Upper Mount Street, cast by the Hammond Lane Foundry of Dublin. Note the shamrocks sprouting at the top. **117** No. 36 Merrion Square South has a foliage pattern based on circles, classical brackets, and the usual openwork iron floor.

117

118

Leningrad, USSR (see p. 31)

118, 119 A Leningrad prospect: the Griboyedov Canal, crossed by the Italian Bridge. The bridge shows an arrangement typical of both Leningrad and Moscow – massive balustrades of cast iron, usually with a central symbolic motif. The heavy railings of the embankment are of the type installed between 1764 and 1790 (see also pl. 122).

119

120 A detail of the railing of the
Garden Bridge, crossing the Moika
River by the Summer Garden,
designed in 1826 by P. Bazaine.
121 Fishing on the Moika
Embankment. The railings, by an
unknown designer, were erected in
1797–1810.

122

Leningrad

122, 123 The Bankovsky (Bank) Bridge crossing the Griboyedov Canal, designed by H. Tretter and built in 1825–26. In the background is the School of Economics.

124, 127 The Demidov Bridge over the Griboyedov Canal, designed by E. Adam in 1834. The bold openwork pattern of anthemia (compare the balcony in pl. 245) is matched in the top of the lamp standard.

125, 126 The same pattern of masks is used on both the Theatre and Malokoniushenny Bridges, at the confluence of the Moika River and Griboyedov Canal, built in 1829–30 to designs by Adam and Tretter. The view of the Theatre Bridge (pl. 125) shows its elaborate lamp bases, with rams' heads and paw feet.

125

124

127

126

128

Leningrad

128, 129 The Pevchesky or Singer's Bridge, crossing the Moika from Palace Square, was built to Adam's design in 1839–40. Above the radiating anthemia and lions' masks, a band of circles echoes those of the Moika railing, seen in the foreground in pl. 128 (compare pl. 121). **130** The Second Garden Bridge over the Moika, 1840, attributed to V. P. Stasov. **131** A modern bridge over the Fontanka at Lermontovsky Prospect suggests bound fasces with Egyptian caps.

129

130

131

132

133

132, 133 The Anichkov Bridge of 1839–41, with its dolphins, seahorses and female tritons (pl. 132), carries Nevsky Prospekt, the grandest street of Leningrad, across the Fontanka River. **134, 135** A freer version of seahorses and trident on the Lieutenant Schmidt Bridge across the vast Neva River. Built in 1842–50 to a design by A. P. Bryullov, creator of the Malachite Room in the Winter Palace, it was renamed after a hero of the 1905 Revolution, and reconstructed after damage in World War II.

134

135

Leningrad

136, 137 Railings around the garden of
the Cathedral of Our Lady of Kazan,
now the Museum of the History of
Religion and Atheism. Both the cathedral
and the railings of 1812, with their powerful
applied motifs and *rinceaux* set between
granite piers, were designed by the great
Neo-classical architect Andrei Voronikhin.

Tsarskoye Selo

138 A view from the Cameron Gallery in the grounds of the Ekaterininsky Palace at Tsarskoye Selo (now Pushkin), about 24 kilometres from Leningrad. The long colonnaded walk, for exercise on wet days, was designed in 1786 for Catherine the Great by her brilliant Anglo-Scottish protégé, Charles Cameron, who worked in the delicate Neo-classical manner of Adam. The elegantly thin balustrade makes a pleasant foreground to a vista of pool and bathing pavilion.

139 Massive Louis XVI revival: the gateway of the Scientific Library of Folk Education. **140** Soviet naval symbolism – anchor, lifebuoy and cables surrounding a radiant star. The position of the ornament, attached to railings, is distinctively Russian: compare pls. 126 and 136. **141** A Neo-classical pattern surrounds the Soviet star on the Kalinin Bridge. The piers are angular paraphrases of fasces.

Moscow, USSR (see pp. 31–32)

142, 143 The Bolshoi Kamenny Bridge (Big Stone Bridge) overlooks the Kremlin on the Moskva River. Its imagery commemorates the revolution and celebrates agriculture and industry: the star is surrounded half by a cog-wheel and half by wheat. The piers again recall fasces.

Paris, France (see pp. 32–33)

144 A Parisian window guard in use, on a modest block of flats in Rue du Chevalier-de-la-Barre, Montmartre, probably *c.* 1900.
145 At the opposite end of the scale, the Baroque classicism of the Louvre is supplemented by heavily patterned ironwork.

Paris

146 A recessed window guard on No. 49 Rue de Seine, on the Left Bank. The Neo-classical design, incorporating an urn, crossed arrows, and a snake swallowing its tail, suggests a date about 1800.

147, 148 One of the vistas created by Haussmann: the Avenue de l'Opéra, built in the 1860s. Many balconies run without interruption across the front of the house. Pl. 148 shows the balustraded walks fronting the mansard roof and top floor at the corner of the Avenue de l'Opéra and Rue Ventadour. (See also pls. 160, 161, 163, 165.)

149

Paris

149-153 A block of flats in Louis XVI style, No. 15 Rue de Solférino on the Left Bank,
has different patterns of cast iron on five levels. Pls. 150–153 show the balconies, from the top floor
down to the first floor (in Paris, usually less important than the second floor). Parisian balustrades
typically have a conspicuous central motif flanked by ornamental scrolls (see pls. 160–165).

150

151

152

Ornements en Fonte de Fer.

BARBEZAT & Cᴵᵉ MAITRES DE FORGES,
SUCCESSEURS DE J. P. V. ANDRÉ.

10. Rue Neuve Ménilmontant. Paris

Pl. 51

BALCONS DE CROISÉE ET GRANDS BALCONS MONTÉS SUR FER.

B. P.

B. M.

N° 28.

N° 26.

N° 24. A.

N° 24. D.

N° 24. B.

N° 24. C.

1850. N.B. Les modèles soulignés ne se font que sur Cᵈᵉ   au Quinzième d'exécution.

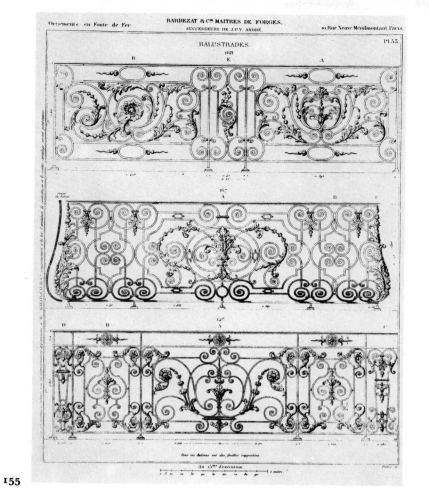

155

156

Plates from the superb catalogue of *fonte de fer* manufactured by Barbezat & Cie. of Paris (see p. 33)

154 Balustrades for single windows and wide balustrades mounted on iron supports, dated 1850. A note at the side threatens would-be copiers with legal action. **155** Balustrades in which the foliage motifs are added separately to the basic casting, to increase the resemblance to wrought iron with *repoussé* details. **156** Handrails, dated 1859. This plate illustrates the high art of casting; the design at the top was commissioned by Napoleon III. **157** A Renaissance balustrade design with fauns and animals, of which a casting was discovered in Utrecht (pl. 182).

157

159

Paris

158 A small balcony on Boulevard Raspail near Rue de Sèvres has a crossed torch and quiver, united by a drape hanging from a bow above, and surrounded by a wreath. Curvaceous scrolls are ornamented by paterae and acanthus leaves in profile – all probably added separately, as advertised in the Barbezat catalogue (pl. 155).
159 A casting resembling wrought iron, illustrated in Barbezat's catalogue.

158

160

160–162 Wide balconies of the mid 19th century, with scrolly designs similar to those in the Barbezat catalogue (pls. 154, 155), at No. 29 and No. 18 Avenue de l'Opéra, and in Place St Germain-des-Prés.

161

162

163

164

165

167

163–165 Shield motifs at No. 26 Avenue de l'Opéra, in the Place St Germain-des-Prés, and again in Avenue de l'Opéra. **166** The window guard of a semi-basement in Avenue Franklin-D.-Roosevelt, a design illustrated in Barbezat's catalogue. **167** Theatrical castings befit the Place du Théâtre Français, at the end of Avenue de l'Opéra. This design even incorporates raised bands, necessary in wrought iron to hold the metal strips together (see pl. 1) but completely artificial in cast iron.

166

Paris

168 A gateway and two alternative fences, from the catalogue of Barbezat & Cie. (see p. 33). **169** *Porte-cochère* in Rue Damrémont. The openwork panels appear in Barbezat's catalogue. **170** Alternative designs for a *porte-cochère*, dated 1855–57, from Barbezat's catalogue.

171-173 Upper and lower panels of a door in Rue Ste Anne, and their model in the Barbezat catalogue.

169

170

171

172

173

561 0.095 (31) **562** 0.133 (22) **563** 0.118 (31) **564** 0.125 (30) **565** 0.092 (30) **566** 0.102 (93) **567** 0.110 (19) **568** 0.068 (18) **569** 0.097 (18) **570** 0.110 (14) **571** 0.099 (31)

572 0.160 (30/96) **573** 0.161 (30/47) **574** 0.153 (23) **575** 0.162 (33) **576** 0.152 (19) **577** 0.116 (29) **578** 0.148 (27) **579** 0.136 (24) **580** 0.160 (30) **581** 0.137 (24) **582** 0.147 (30/142)

583 0.127 (21/149) **584** 0.213 (41) **585** 0.200 (25) **586** 0.203 (27) **587** 0.212 (28) **588** 0.187 **589** 0.188 (23) **590** 0.185 (21/17) **591** 0.184 (24) **592** 0.200 (22) **593** 0.197 (35)

594 0.227 (43) **595** 0.201 (23) **596** 0.237 (27) **597** 0.222 (26) **598** 0.167 (40) **599** 0.213 (34) **600** 0.210 (33) **601** 0.221 (39) **602** 0.220 (38) **603** 0.195 (134) **604** 0.163

605 0.195 (18/134) **606** 0.216 (27) **607** 0.223 (25) **608** 0.245 (40) **609** 0.240 (24) **610** 0.230 (64) **611** 0.249 (35) **612** 0.236 (43) **613** 0.240 (27) **614** 0.246 (41) **615** 0.163 (25/163)

616 0.230 (25/148) **617** 0.239 (27) **618** 0.247 (42) **619** 0.240 (41) **620** 0.254 (33) **621** 0.245 (66) **622** 0.252 (30) **623** 0.253 (40) **624** 0.248 (40) **625** 0.253 (47) **626** 0.158 (28/158)

616 0.276 **617** 0.253 **618** 0.246 **619** 0.279 **620** 0.262 **621** 0.246 **622** 0.260 **623** 0.269 **624** 0.282/0.321 **625** 0.272

174 The astonishing variety of cast iron picket heads available is illustrated by the catalogue of the Société Anonyme des Hauts Fourneaux & Fonderies du Val d'Osne, a successor to Barbezat & Cie.: this is only one of three pages of *lances et fleurons*.

Paris

175 No. 7 Rond Point des Champs Elysées is a detached house, a rare thing in Paris. It shows the beauty of the expensively built 19th-century Parisian dwelling, with French windows leading on to curving balconies in 18th-century style. **176** Eiffel's iron tower, built for the Exhibition of 1889, symbolizes an era of structural use of cast iron. It is seen across the Seine from the Pont Alexandre III, with its magnificent lanterns, built for the Exhibition of 1900.

176

175

Amsterdam, The Netherlands
(see p. 34)

177 No. 592 Herengracht is typical of many houses in which a *stoep* rises from pavement level to the main entrance door. A door below leads to a semi-basement. The baluster posts, of a plain type which is also used in Amsterdam, with variations, for bridges, incorporate Ionic capitals.
178 The *stoep* railings of the Nederlandsche Middenstands Spaarbank in Herengracht consist of wide ornamental castings of early 18th-century character. **179** A magnificently cast lamp standard on Nieuwe Zijds Voorburgwal, behind the Royal Palace. It bears inscriptions stating that it was designed by M. G. Tetar van Elven and cast by Dixon & Co. of Amsterdam in 1844.

Utrecht, The Netherlands (see p. 34)

180 The façade of the Vlaer and Kol Bank on Oudegracht, of 1836–39, has a loggia with cast iron caryatids dimly based on those of the Erechtheion in Athens. The balcony railing above them displays a less rustic Neo-classicism. **181, 182** Castings from designs by the Parisian firm of Barbezat & Cie. (see p. 33): a cellar grating at No. 65 Nieuwegracht and a balcony at No. 20 Maliebaan, showing young fauns and animals (compare pl. 157 and p. 33, fig. 6). **183** A fanlight at No. 53 Nieuwegracht incorporates a lamp which shines both outwards and inwards. **184** Delicately cast ventilating grilles in the doors of a butcher's shop at No. 78 Nieuwegracht.

181

182

183

184

185

Delft, The Netherlands

185, 186 A cast iron bridge and *stoep* railing in
Voorstraat.

De Bilt, The Netherlands

187, 188 In this village, about 5 kilometres from
Utrecht, a restaurant has a double-storeyed
veranda that recalls New Orleans (pl. 299), while
Sandwyk, a mansion of 1846, shows two verandas –
one double-storeyed, and one single-storeyed
but polygonal.

189 A very useful Dutch cast iron device, set in a door,
which allows the householder to see and converse with
a visitor without opening the door.

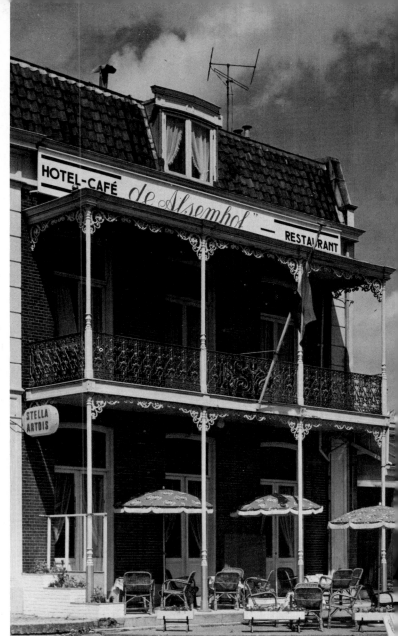

187

188

189

Lisbon, Portugal (see pp. 34–35)

190 It is impossible not to be aware of the balconies of Lisbon, especially in older parts of the city: the lamps with their cast iron brackets are a feature of the narrow *travessas*, as are the narrow balconettes for individual windows that jut out over the street. **191** A gently bowed balcony sits against a tiled façade. The pattern is an attractive one, the grooving of the scrolls contributing to its effectiveness. **192** Balconies and ceramic tiles in the Avenida da Liberdade. The railing pattern used – both flat and curved – is similar to several designs by the Parisian firm of Barbezat & Cie. (see pl. 154, no. 28, and pl. 503).

193

194

195

Lisbon

Gustave Eiffel's street lift of cast iron (see p. 35)

(see p. 35)

193 The lift has many varied Gothic patterns, and the windows are of different design at each level. **194** Detail of the third tier window (true 'wind-eyes'). **195** The tall balustrade of the expanded landing stage, which is supported below by huge cast consoles. It overlooks the houses of the lower part of the city that rise in tiers to the castle. **196** A spiral staircase climbing to two higher levels.

196

197

Athens, Greece (see p. 35)

197 A balcony on the Hotel Grande-Bretagne, formerly
the Palais Dimitriou, built in 1842–43 by the Neo-
classical architect Theophil von Hansen, sets
the style of the ironwork of Athens in its 'Greek
Revival' mood; human heads and winged torsos,
equine legs and hoofs, fanciful fish tails and fins,
illustrate man's desire for forms of locomotion on land,
sea and in the air. 198 The Acropolis from Eolou
Street. 199 No. 24A Panos Street: in the balcony, a
swan with a tail of volutes appears below a Greek key
pattern.

200

201

202

Athens

200 The loggia of the Supreme Court building, formerly the house of the archaeologist Schliemann, discoverer of Troy. Here in 1878 Hansen's pupil Ziller still, appropriately, used a Greek Revival balustrade: a central vase is flanked by gorgeous griffins, whose tail feathers merge into acanthus-like foliage. **201** A winged woman gives rise to spreading volutes with acanthus-like leaves, which in turn support swans whose necks echo the curves in the design. **202** At No. 20 Apostolou Pavlou a vase and double-headed eagle are flanked by fire-breathing dragon-like creatures. The width of the panel and the tendency to frame a central decorative feature above and below the principal panel are features of the ironwork of Athens.

Spain

203, 204 Spain is a country of wrought iron; but these glazed suntraps, or *miradors*, in Toledo (pl. 203) and Madrid use cast iron for an openwork pattern or a fringe at the top, combined with wrought iron balustrades.

205

Italy

205, 206 Rome: one of the branching cast iron lamp standards in Bernini's piazza in front of St Peter's; and an archivolt in Piazza Navona, which is similar to French designs (pl. 170) but is associated with the former Spanish Church in Rome. Its inscription reads: 'REAL PAT. DE SANTIAGO Y MONSERRAT. AÑO 1870'.

207 Venice: a balcony in flowing Rococo style at No. 4191 Riva degli Schiavoni, facing the Bacino di San Marco.

206

207

Austria

208 Unusual, rather delicate patterns of cast iron are to be found in some small towns in Austria. The bracket is of a standard Neo-classical type (compare pl. 12).

209 Vienna: the imposing fence of the Neue Hofburg, 1881–1914, along Dr Karl Renner-Ring.

208

209

Copenhagen, Denmark

210 The fence around Frederiks Kirke, Bredgade, near the Amalienborg Palace – probably a combination of cast and wrought iron. The church, begun in 1749, was not completed until 1875–94. In its churchyard, seen here, are statues of eminent Danish churchmen.

211

Stockholm, Sweden

211 A doorway in the old town with cast iron panels (compare Paris, pl. 169). The central panel, like a mid 19th-century book illustration, shows a couple in Northern Renaissance costume. **212** Torch-bearers on the Enskilda Bank, No. 8 Kungsträdgårdsgatan. **213** Railings and gates of the Army Museum in Riddargatan. All the motifs are suitably warlike: the railings have the form of spears, the gate piers of fasces with axes (symbolic of war); on the gates are thunderbolts, while on the outside, not seen here, the pier bases display flaming bombs and grenades.

212

213

214

New York (see pp. 38–40)

214 The Haughwout Building, one of the finest and best preserved of the city's cast iron buildings. Built in 1856 to the design of J. P. Gaynor and made by Badger's Architectural Iron Works (see pls. 216, 322), its Venetian arcades were originally painted a light colour to imitate stone. It served as shop, warehouse and factory for E. V. Haughwout, a dealer in luxury goods who rivalled Tiffany. (Photo Historic American Buildings Survey/Cervin Robinson)

215 The frontispiece of Daniel D. Badger's *Illustrations of Iron Architecture, Made by the Architectural Iron Works of the City of New York*, 1865, shows the firm's office (background) and factory. In the basement, the picture shows casting on the left, and smiths at work on the right. Above, in the galleries, are rolling presses (the firm made its name with iron shutters), polishing wheels and lathes; on the top floor, finishing touches are given to what look like window frames (compare pl. 326). In the foreground, designers and clients discuss drawings. (Reproduced from the collection of the Library of Congress, Washington, D.C.)

216

217

New York catalogues

216, 217 From Daniel D. Badger's *Illustrations of Iron Architecture, Made by the Architectural Iron Works of the City of New York*, 1865 (see pp. 39–40). Pl. 216 shows details of the façade of the Cary Building in New York, designed in 1856 by Gamaliel King and John Kellum using existing components made by Badger's firm. With its iron plates imitating rusticated stone, the Cary Building still stands at the corner of Chambers and Reade Street and is probably the oldest iron building in the city. In pl. 217 we see 'Verandah and Verandah Railings', one of only two such domestic designs in the catalogue.
218 Figure 76W from *Iron Manufactures of the New York Wire Railing Company*, 1857 (see p. 37). Verandas with the same columns and balustrade appear on houses of 1858 at Savannah, Georgia, and the balustrade pattern is used for fencing in the Garden District of New Orleans. **219** Railings, from a catalogue of John B. Wickersham's New York Wire Railing Works. The date is unknown, but the price for wide castings will be envied. **220** Page 57 from Fiske's *Illustrated Catalogue of Iron Railings* showing well-designed and beautifully cast specimens, called Fuller's Patent Railing. Pattern B 13 was designed as grave fencing – hence the weeping willow.

218

219

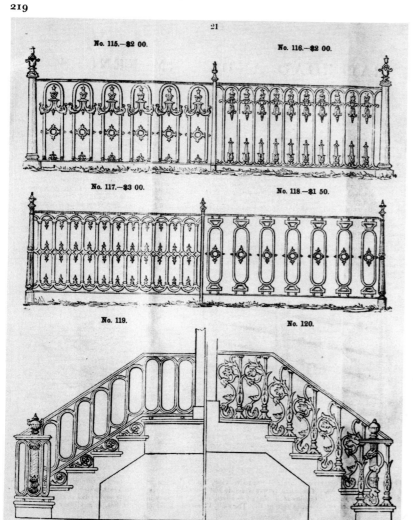

21

No. 115.—$2 00.   No. 116.—$2 00.

No. 117.—$3 00.   No. 118.—$1 50.

No. 119.   No. 120.

220

FULLER'S PATENT RAILING

No. B 10 PATTERN.
3 feet 6 inches high.

No B 11 PATTERN.   No B 12 PATTERN.   No B 13 PATTERN.

221

221 Staircase railing terminating in a griffin, from the *Illustrated Catalogue 'N'* of the J. L. Mott Iron Works, New York, 1891. The firm was established in 1828, and produced many fine catalogues. 222 Title page of a catalogue of A. B. & W. T. Westervelt's foundry in New York. These sprightly Victorian Gothic finials are undated.

New York

223 Railings on a row of brownstone houses. The griffins are similar to those shown in Mott's catalogue (pl. 221), and the design also recalls the railings of the Dakota Apartments on West 72nd Street, of 1884. Most of the houses here had deteriorated as they became overcrowded tenements, but they are capable of noble restoration.

CAST AND WROUGHT IRON
FINIALS, BANNERETS AND CROSSES
MANUFACTURED BY
A. B. & W. T. WESTERVELT,
102 CHAMBERS STREET, COR. CHURCH,
NEW YORK.

IRON FINIAL AND BANNERET. No. 196.

IRON FINIAL AND BANNERET. No. 197.

IRON FINIAL AND BANNERET. No. 195.

222

New York

224 Large openwork urns capped with pineapples (symbols of welcome), and resting on truncated Doric columns, flank the steps of No. 56 West 10th Street, built in 1832. Exquisite doorways are a feature of many New York houses; that on the right shows delicate iron patterns in sidelights and overdoor. **225** A strong fence of haphazard but pleasant arrangement borders a basement and rises with a few steps to the entrance of No. 43 West 12th Street, Greenwich Village. Note the large newel posts. Part of the railing is missing. **226** Nos. 330–326 East 18th Street. Flat openwork columns of an attractive *rinceau* design support the floor of this row of covered balconies. On the balconies flat filigree columns, friezes of geometrical design and large brackets form a type of ornamentation seen commonly in New Orleans and occasionally in other cities in the United States. The steps leading up to the balconies are made of cast iron. The railings of steps and balconies are of the same design, but on the balconies the panels are closely spaced.

225

226

227

230

228

229   232

New York

227 A typical row of residences in Chelsea, Nos. 404–418 West 20th Street, built in the 1830s and 40s. Note the massive newel posts in the foreground, capped by pineapples. The anthemion motif features in both fence and balustrade. 228, 229 Nos. 20 and 21 Washington Square North, c. 1831. The balcony of No. 21, seen above its fence capped by a bold honeysuckle design, has small anthemion motifs concentrated in circles with meander borders. The other components of the balustrade recall the balconies of Upper Woburn Place in London (pl. 12).
230 A fence of Washington Square North, 1830s. Acanthus leaves are ingeniously given a lyre shape; paterae, meanders and two forms of curling anthemion complete the design. 231, 232 No. 107 in Waverley Place, an extension of Washington Square North, also built in the 1830s. The rail of the basement area has a small subtle anthemion pattern, and the other ironwork is based on classical motifs as well – meander (on the stairs), arrows and masks (on the balcony). The arrangement of the ironwork is similar to that of many London houses, yet the difference, in pattern and in such features as the curling newel posts (seen also in pl. 234), can be spotted at a glance.

231

New York

233, 234, 236 Nos. 3 and 4 Gramercy Park West have verandas and porches on the raised entrance floor with broad openwork columns and deep friezes with brackets. The houses were built in the late 1830s as private homes: they are now elegant and much sought-after high-rental apartments. A similar arrangement to the swirling newel post of No. 3 (pl. 234) is to be seen at the foot of the stairs of the Law Courts at Melbourne, in Australia. **235** Fence and gate of Gramercy Park, laid out *c.* 1831. The park is the only private one in Manhattan, owners of surrounding buildings and some tenants alone having keys to this gate.

234

236

237

238

New York

237 A turtle in the ironwork of No. 231 East 48th Street, one of twenty houses built in the 1860s and known as Turtle Bay Gardens. Rehabilitated in 1920, the houses were given new railings topped by this appropriate symbol. **238** Stair of the University Club, 1 West 54th Street, by McKim, Mead and White, 1897–99.

Boston, Massachusetts

Beacon Hill (see p. 41)

239 A view up Chestnut Street, with No. 23 in the foreground. Greek meanders occupy the faces of the hollow gateposts, while at No. 23 anthemion motifs and stars adorn the balcony balustrade (compare pl. 258), and an attractive console helps to support the balcony. Beyond are two bows, typical of Beacon Hill, with curved balconies.

Boston

Beacon Hill (see p. 41)

240 No. 20 Louisburg Square. Note the pineapple finial,
symbol of welcome, on the corner post of the steps leading
down to the basement. The entrance floor has a bow with a
parallel iron balustrade of Neo-classical design. The square
was built up in the 1820s and 1830s. **241** No. 1 Louisburg
Square. The three component patterns, based on palmette
and anthemion, are similar to illustrations in Cottingham's
The Smith and Founder's Director, published in London in 1824
(see pl. 2, no. 1 and pl. 3, bottom right). The anthemion or
honeysuckle motif is extremely common in Boston, and
appears with many variations (pls. 242, 244, 245, 248–50).
242 Six different anthemion designs are seen in this Beacon
Hill fence that fronts an attractive portico with delicate
freestanding Ionic columns. The marked incurving of the
petals of the flowers is characteristic of Boston.

244

243

Boston

Beacon Hill (see p. 41)

243 No. 43 Mount Vernon Street has a
small iron fence and a long balcony
with a slatted floor on consoles. **244** At
No. 61 Mount Vernon Street a *rinceau*
pattern borders the walk to the front
door. Supported by heavy posts, it sits
quite well with the gate of different
design that shows the Boston fondness
for curling anthemia. **245** Nos. 71–67
Hancock Street, near the State House.
Tall narrow panels with anthemion
bases protect basements and steps,
while stylized filigree anthemion and
palmette fill the balustrades. The
openwork anthemion recalls
Leningrad (pls. 124, 127).

245

246 In the balustrade of No. 61 Beacon Street a Grecian figure of the goddess Ceres, holding a cornucopia, is flanked by a grapevine pattern, and then by wide panels with central anthemia from which arise volutes of acanthus foliage (compare pl. 265), framed by bands of interlace. **247** Three houses in Beacon Street near Joy Street recall London terrace houses (pl. 48). Their roofed balconies, rare in Boston, are of a fairly plain late Georgian design that contrasts with more exuberant later American ironwork (pls. 274, 293).

247

248

249

Boston

Three versions of the anthemion motif in the Beacon Hill area (see p. 41). **248** No. 91 Pinckney Street shows an alternation of anthemion and tulip or palmette motifs. **249** No. 7 Louisburg Square, *c.* 1830. The anthemion is distorted but still recognizable as a central motif amongst leaves and flowers. **250** At No. 93 Pinckney Street the designer has produced a curious set of flowing variations on the same motif, stylized far beyond its classical models.

Salem, Massachusetts

251 The anthemion design characteristic of Beacon Hill appears in a number of variations on the massive fence and hollow square posts of the Pingree House, designed in 1804 by Samuel McIntire.

252

253

Boston

The New South End (see p. 41)

252 The bows and high stoops characteristic of this area, begun *c.* 1850.
Iron fences protect the front gardens. There are no balconies, and
the anthemion pattern has been replaced by exuberant *rinceaux* that
seem sometimes to ascend (as here), sometimes to spill down the steps
(pl. 256). **253** Paired steps are divided by *rinceaux* and bordered by
Gothic arches. **254** The classical type of baluster is not uncommon in
the South End: see also pl. 256.

254

255

257

255, 257 The ironwork of No. 58 Chester Square, unusually ornate for
Boston, consists of a curved veranda following the bow of the house and
bearing an open balcony. Pl. 255 shows the filigree columns, brackets
and frieze, pl. 257 the elaborate arrangement of the veranda's
balustrade, where brackets brace the bottoms of the columns – an
uncommon feature. **256** Some façades are flat with oriel windows.
The stair railings in the foreground have the familiar *rinceaux*, but
beyond there are heavy balusters (compare pl. 254). The fence has a
Gothic pattern.

256

258

Boston

259 The bowed balcony of a house on Bunker Hill Square is reminiscent of Regency balconies in England. The balusters of fence and balcony are of the same design, incorporating a star (alluding to the flag?); larger stars appear at the centre of the unusual stair balusters.

258, 261 Balustrades in Commonwealth Avenue, in the Back Bay (p. 42). In pl. 258 a central garlanded urn, suggestive of Adam or of the more angular Louis XVI style, is flanked by three types of baluster. The wider ones recall a design in Cottingham's *Director*, published in London in 1824. Pl. 261 shows an unmistakably French design: the laurel leaves and tassels on a geometric background are similar to balconies in the mid 19th-century catalogue of Barbezat of Paris (p. 33).

260, 262 A summer house and railings, from the *Illustrated Catalogue of Iron Work* of Chase Brothers & Co., 15 Winter Street, Boston. Compare the summer house with pl. 287, and the upper railing with pl. 308. (The Metropolitan Museum of Art, New York)

259

260

261

262

Philadelphia, Pennsylvania

Society Hill (see p. 42)

263, 264 The early 19th-century Bishop Stevens House resembles a British terrace house, but the steps and door surrounds are of white marble. The balustrade is represented in exact detail in Cottingham's *The Smith and Founder's Director*, published in London in 1824 (see pl. 4). **265, 266** In Society Hill the marble stoops with their cast iron embellishments project out into the brick pavement. In the foreground a lyre pattern contrasts with the anthemion and acanthus motifs of the landing. The latter is similar to a pattern seen in Boston (the side panels in pl. 246). The lyre is a feature of Philadelphia ironwork: in pl. 266 a lyre with grapes and acanthus leaves is flanked by arrows.

264

263

265

266

267

Baltimore, Maryland (see pp. 42–43)

267 The grand spiral staircase of the Peabody Institute. The balustrade, cast by Bartlett, Robbins & Co. in the 1870s, has two *rinceau* layers.

268, 269 The mascots of the Baltimore firm of Bartlett, Robbins & Co., seen on the cover of a catalogue issued after 1866 (when the name changed from Hayward, Bartlett & Co.), and standing outside the offices of the Bartlett-Hayward Division of the Koppers Company in Baltimore today. The dogs, cast by one of the original partners of the firm who was a keen duck-hunter, are representations of Sailor and Canton, brought to America in 1807 and regarded as the primogenitors of the Newfoundland Chesapeake Bay dog. According to company legend, they were once removed: 'Hard times followed, which some credited directly to the absence of the dogs. They were found and replaced, . . . and signify the firm's continuing prosperity.'

270, 271 The Peabody Institute Library, 1875–78, by E. G. Lind. The book stacks rise on six floors around a large central well. All the structural material that can be seen is iron, manufactured by Bartlett, Robbins & Co. The printed specification survives (see p. 43). (Reproduced with permission from a photograph of the George Peabody Department, Enoch Pratt Free Library, Baltimore)

268

269

270

271

Baltimore

272 Design for two-storeyed veranda of cast iron, from a catalogue of Bartlett, Robbins & Co. (see p. 43). A detail shows the convolvulus or morning glory pattern of the columns and frieze. Elements of this design appear on houses in the city: see pls. 273–275. (Reproduced with permission from the George Peabody Department, Enoch Pratt Free Library, Baltimore).

273 Two-storey verandas in East Lombard Street. A convolvulus pattern is seen on columns and friezes, three bunches of grapes form a fringe on each arch, and C- and S-scrolls contribute to the brackets. The pattern is shown in pl. 272 with different balustrades, and without the tiny rosettes in the brackets.

272

274, 275 Another arrangement of delicate castings. A *rinceau* design occupies the greater part of the balustrade. Vine leaves form an unusual fringe, not seen elsewhere, in front of the upper part of the frieze. This arrangement may also be discerned in pl. 272. The brackets are the same as those shown in pl. 273, with small rosettes. The close resemblance to the pattern advertised by Bartlett, Robbins & Co. (pl. 272) suggests that this local firm designed and cast the ironwork.

274

275

276

277

278

Georgetown, Washington, D.C.

(see pp. 43–44)

277 A basement window guard at No. 2803 P Street incorporates the eagle and shield of the United States.

279 A 20th-century house follows tradition in modified form.

276, 278 In Georgetown complete stoops of cast iron jut out over the brick pavements. The steps of No. 1403 O Street (pl. 276) are particularly wide, and descend at right angles to the house, as in Holland (pl. 177). The risers have an angular geometrical pattern until they reach the landing, which is surrounded by a lush *rinceau* (compare pl. 278). A combination of cast iron and wrought iron, used here for the balustrade, is common in Georgetown. The window guard is of cast iron. The risers of the steps shown in pl. 278 have an ornate *rinceau* pattern with at its centre a star (seen most clearly in the shadow) – presumably, as in Boston (pl. 259), a patriotic emblem.

279

Charleston, South Carolina (see pp. 44–45)

280 The Edmonston-Alston House, 21 East Battery, has a grand three-storey 'piazza', the characteristic Charleston veranda running along the side of the house. It was built *c.* 1828 and enriched after 1838. The tall cast iron roofed balcony of late Georgian type, fronted by a balustrade patterned with anthemion, volutes and circles, and supported by massive consoles, is one of the later enrichments.

Charleston (see pp. 44–45)

281 The Pre-Revolutionary John Rutledge House, 116 Broad Street, was given its ornate ironwork in the mid 19th century. The filigree columns have one, two or four sides. Horizontal bars suggest supports for banners or flags. With its cast iron fence, window guards and double curved balustraded steps leading to the veranda, it is one of the most flamboyant houses we have seen. (In the foreground is the late Samuel Gaillard Stoney, author of *This is Charleston*) **282** The brave display of ironwork of the first-floor balcony of the Ladson House, 8 Meeting Street, has filigree columns, friezes and brackets similar to those in Baltimore (pls. 272–275). A matching unroofed balcony, with delicate consoles, is attached at the side. The house dates from 1806, the balconies probably from 1821. **283** The façade of the Dock Street Theatre, 135 Church Street, is that of the Planters Hotel of 1809, restored during the Depression. Balusters and columns are based on the *rinceau*. The ornate consoles of the lobby are of carved mahogany. **284, 285** St John Hotel, 115 Meeting Street, *c.* 1853. Pl. 285 shows the view from the left-hand end of the balcony, down Meeting Street to St Michael's Church. The grapevine pattern of the ironwork is reminiscent of New Orleans (pl. 297). The hotel has since been rebuilt, as a replica of the old.

282

283

284

285

Charleston (see pp. 44–45)

286 No. 37 Meeting Street, a Pre-Revolutionary house with later ironwork. A small roofed balcony over the doorway is recessed between two massive bows which constitute the front of the house – an unusual arrangement. While the balcony is of cast iron, the fence and gate are of wrought iron, more common in Charleston than in most American cities.

287

287 The balcony of No. 1 Prioleau Street, an Ante-Bellum building, with geometrical patterns of ironwork (compare a Boston design, pl. 260). The design of balustrades, columns and frieze differs from the lush patterns shown in some previous plates, while the curving-roofed form suggests late Georgian influence. The central panel of the balustrade is unfortunately missing. **288** The cast iron fences of Charleston are worthy of study. As befits a churchyard, panels of Gothic design are inset at intervals in the fence of the Huguenot Church, built in the 1840s.

286

New Orleans, Louisiana

The Vieux Carré (see pp. 45–46)

289–292 The Pontalba Buildings, two identical rows of shops and flats built in 1849–50, flank Jackson Square at the heart of the French Quarter. (In the foreground in pl. 289 is the square's cast iron railing, 1851). Iron pillars form an arcade at street level; above them are two tiers of ironwork, the upper unroofed. The balustrades and ventilator grilles at the top have the intertwined letters A and P as a central motif, for Micaela Almonester, Baroness Pontalba, builder of the houses. She is said to have designed the monogram herself; Waldemar Appolonius Talen carved the model, which was cast in New York. The Pontalba designs appear among recastings made by the Lorio Iron Works of New Orleans (pl. 290, lower row), who have made reproductions as well as their own designs since 1905. Among designs shown here – Neo-classical and Gothic – is a winged hourglass, no. 104, intended for grave fences (see pl. 321). From the rounded corners of the eastern Pontalba Building one can look across Jackson Square to the twin Pontalba Building (pl. 291), and in the opposite direction (pl. 292) along unroofed and roofed balconies in St Ann Street, showing the unique character of New Orleans ironwork.

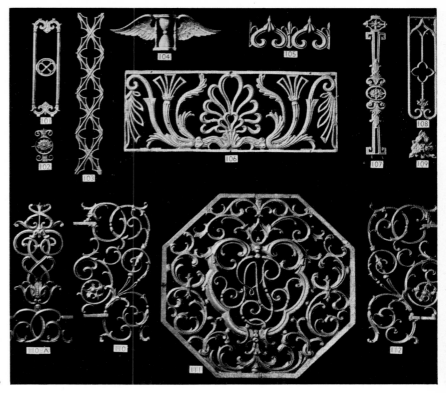

290

291   292

New Orleans

The Vieux Carré (see p. 45) (see p. 45)

293, 294 The climax of the New Orleans style: the three Miltenberger Houses, 900 Royal Street, built in 1838, and given their galleries in the 1850s. Three tiers are capped by a small balcony on the fourth storey. The decorative motifs are oak leaves and acorns – with grapevines, the most common design in the city.

293

Characteristic oak and grapevine ornament

294 The oak pattern of the Miltenberger Houses. **295** An oak frieze and column with grapevine cresting. **296** Grapevine frieze and column. **297** A different grapevine column and balusters.

294

295

296

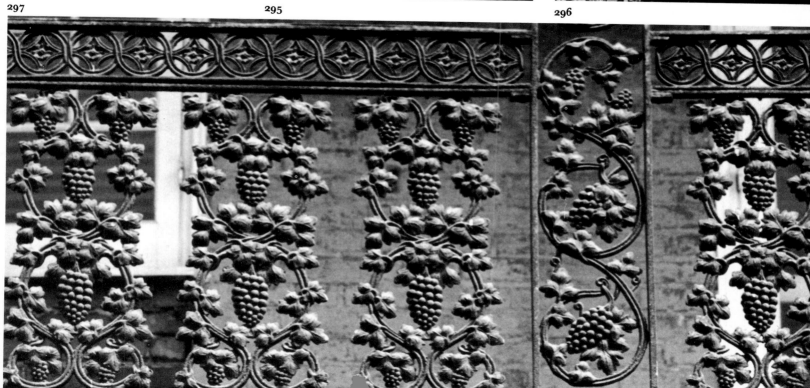

297

New Orleans

The classic Vieux Carré theme (see p. 45)

298–300 Tall slender columns, set near the edge of the footpath, support roofed galleries of cast iron. The street level occasionally has an iron frieze (in the foreground in pl. 298, also pl. 293). The ironwork may be on two or three storeys, and the upper storey may be unroofed (pl. 298, right). All the galleries seen here have different patterns of castings: that in pl. 300 is the familiar oak (pls. 293–295). The main balustrade pattern in pl. 298 reappears in the Garden District (pls. 310, 314). Balconies are occasionally of wood (pl. 299, left).

300

298
299

Variations on the theme

301 A cantilevered balcony with cast iron balustrade and a roof supported by consoles faces the street, while at the side of the house a balcony with wooden balustrade and columns overlooks a courtyard. Originally a smaller gate would have opened from street to courtyard. **302** A pair of similar houses is fronted by garden plots and iron fences, unusual in the Vieux Carré. In addition to filigree columns, balustrades, brackets and friezes, the house on the right has a crest along the roof. **303** A small cantilevered balcony on a house in Esplanade Avenue, of 1856, with cast iron consoles and a recessed roof with a fringe. The balustrade panels, with a Neo-classical dancing child, are unusual.

301

302

303

305

304

New Orleans

The Garden District (see p. 46)

304 The balcony of Hinderer's Iron Works, 1780 Prytania Street (see p. 47). The main ironworks was established in 1864. The columns and frieze have a grapevine pattern seen in the Vieux Carré (pl. 296). On the balcony is a garden bench of grape and acanthus design made by Hinderer's.
305 This symmetrical gate cresting is illustrated in Hinderer's file 15c.
306 No. 1315 First Street, built about 1870, has a complete ornamental iron front that breaks forward in the centre and includes slender cylindrical columns. Such façades are very common in Melbourne (see, for instance, pls. 386, 405), and no other counterpart was seen in New Orleans. The frieze is the same as that of No. 1448 Fourth Street (pl. 310), while the balusters are common to a number of countries. Heavy gates and iron fences of this type are a feature of the Garden District (pls. 314, 315, 317).

307

308

New Orleans

The Garden District (see p. 46)

307–310 No. 1448 Fourth Street, the Alfred Jay Moran or Short-Moran House, built in 1859 to designs by Henry Howard. The famous cornstalk fence was furnished by Wood and Miltenberger, New Orleans agent of the Philadelphia Foundry of Wood and Perot, and restored in 1950. Pls. 307 and 308 show the massive corner post and the fence itself, a variant of 'rustic' design (compare pl. 262). The heavy posts have a base of pumpkins, and morning glory entwines them to reach up to the corncob finials. The balusters are modelled on maize plants. A similar fence and gate may be seen at No. 915 Royal Street in the Vieux Carré. The house, seen in the background in pl. 308, has two-storey iron verandas at the front and at the side, the latter curved on a generous bow and with delicate castings (pl. 310). Pl. 309 shows the filigree ironwork of the columns, which has the same pattern as the frieze. The baluster pattern occurs elsewhere (pls. 298, 314).

311

312
313

314

New Orleans

The Garden District (see p. 46)

311-313 The Thomas Jordan House, 1415 Third Street, late 1850s. The front (at the left in pl. 311) has iron balustrades of a bizarre classical/Romanesque form (pl. 312), while at the side there is a remarkable lacy display: unique features are the pairing of the wide filigree columns, and their spandrels from which hang iron tassels. The frieze pattern is that of the columns (as in pl. 310), and the motifs are echoed in the cresting.

314 The Harris-Crassons House, 2127 Prytania Street, by James Calrow, built in 1857–58, is a 'raised cottage' (see p. 46). Of the two ornate iron patterns, on veranda and stairs, that of the veranda is one we have already seen (pls. 298, 310), but used upside-down.

315 The Payne-Strachan House, 1134 First Street, 1849–50: the same formula of columns linked by iron balustrades, here on two storeys.

315

316

318

316 No. 2627 Coliseum Street, in the
Garden District, contrasts with the
previous formal houses. The columns, and
the frieze in the background, are of the
grapevine pattern (pls. 296, 304).
317 No. 1749 Lower Coliseum Street,
1847, has a wide bow on each floor, heavy
stucco architrave and lintels, and columns
with Ionic and Corinthian capitals. The
balustrades, which as usual front the
upper storey, have wide balusters that are
symmetrical in both directions.
318 A spiral staircase at No. 1415
Exposition Boulevard. The risers have a
basketwork pattern and the panels in the
gate are the same as the balusters of the
stair.

320

319 The base of an iron column from the Church of the
Immaculate Conception in Baronne Street, designed by
Father John Gambiaso and T. E. Giraud, 1851–57. The
present building, built in 1929–30 after a fire, incorporates
the original cast iron columns and pews. **320** The grand
stair of Teamsters' Building, Elysian Fields. The
anthemion, so common in Boston and so rare in New
Orleans, has reappeared, and the risers also show Greek
motifs.
321 The Durel tomb in St Louis Cemetery No. 2 (see
pp. 46–47). The winged hourglasses symbolize the fleeting
hours of life (compare pl. 290).

321

San Francisco, California (see pp. 47–48)

322 Probably the first cast iron façade in the city, long since disappeared: the Savings and Loan Society, Clay Street, designed by J. P. Gaynor (see also pl. 214) and built in 1870. On the left is an ornate balcony with the same *rinceau* pattern as that of the Dock Street Theatre in Charleston (pl. 283). (Photograph by courtesy of the California Historical Society, San Francisco)

322

323

324

325

323-325 The iron façade of the Trust Department of the American Trust Company, seen intact and during dismantling in 1959 (p. 47). It was erected between May 1873 and March 1874 for the Bank of London and San Francisco. The tiers of columns show the classic orders, Doric, Ionic and Corinthian; flowered scrolls in panels appear on each floor, and above the windows are heads that include angels, bears and eagles. The entrance, with Atlantes and pillars bearing the foundry's name – 'Hinckley & Co. Fulton Foundry San Francisco 1873' – is now in the San Francisco Maritime Museum, and the ornate window unit above it is at Oakland.

San Francisco (see p. 47)

326 The Kneedler-Fauchère Building, 451–461 Jackson Street, originally the Hotaling liquor warehouse, a complete iron-fronted structure built about 1860. The well preserved ground floor shows, as Badger in New York pointed out, how cast iron could frame large areas of glass, lighting up the store inside – a practical consideration in the days before electricity. The iron pillars bear the mark of the California Foundry, San Francisco. **327** The Hallidie Building, 130 Sutter Street, built in 1918, has a curtain wall of iron and glass in front of the main fabric of the building. The ironwork includes an unexpected touch of Early Christian art in the motif of birds flanking a vase, but the castings lack crispness.

Columbia, California (see p. 48)

328 The Wells Fargo Express Building, built in this Gold Rush town after the fire of 1857. The windows and doors have iron shutters to protect against the spread of fire. The cast iron of the balcony was shipped from Troy, New York, and hauled to Columbia by mules.

327

New South Wales &c.

21

32

FLETCHER BENNETT & FREW
NEWTOWN

54

REGISTERED 15 OCT 1880

55

56

89

90

91

92

93

94

95

96

97

98

114

120

121

131

132

133

134

135

144

152

154

159

Australia and New Zealand

330

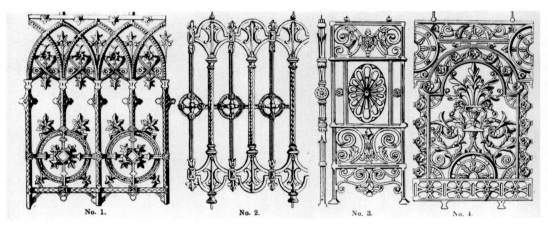

331

New South Wales designs (pp. 52, 65–67)

329 Designs registered in 1879–84. (Here, and in pls. 332, 335 and 338, the following information is given by columns, from left to right, reading down: registration number, date, and name of applicant.)

(1) *16* 17.12.1879, D. Livingstone; *21* 4.3.1880, G. & J. Fletcher (trading as G. Fletcher & Son); *32* 18.5.1880, D. & R. Bradford (see pl. 360, and compare pls. 334, 360); *54, 55* 15.10.1880, P. P. Fletcher, T. O. Bennett & G. Frew (trading as Fletcher, Bennett & Frew).

(2) *56* 15.10.1880, Fletcher, Bennett & Frew; *89–92* 16.8.1881, *idem* (for no. 89 see pls. 424, 426, for no. 90, pl. 332).

(3) *93–98* 16.8.1881, Fletcher, Bennett & Frew; (no. 96 also appears in Victoria and South Australia: pls. 332, 336); *114* 18.7.1882, D. & R. Bradford.

(4) *120* 18.10.1882, J. Crase; *121* 10.11.1882, Joseph & Henry Juleff (also registered in Queensland in 1887 by Crase & Wilson: pl. 338, no. 40); *131–134* 6.9.1883, A. T. Rees (trading as A. T. Rees & Co.; no. 132 appears in pl. 363).

(5) *135* 6.9.1883, A. T. Rees & Co. (see pl. 363); *144* 24.4.1884, D. & R. Bradford (see pl. 357); *145* 16.5.1884, J. Crase; *152* 21.6.1884, *idem*; *154* 15.7.1884, *idem*; *159* 3.9.1884, A. H. Brown.

330, 331 Friezes, brackets and balustrades from the catalogue of Holdsworth MacPherson, wholesale ironmongers. The firm first appeared in Sydney directories in 1882. In 1928 it became Keep, MacPherson Ltd, and after 1932 it disappeared from the directory. Pattern no. 10 resembles that seen in pl. 329 (no. 144) and pl. 357; no. 11 and balustrade no. 3 will be seen in Melbourne (pl. 407); no. 13 appears in pl. 360, and no. 4 in pl. 368; it and no. 1 have echoes in a Melbourne catalogue (pl. 334, nos. 14 and 8).

Victoria designs (see pp. 52, 67–69)

332 Designs registered in 1874–87 (see note on pl. 329)

(1) *124* 9.10.1874, John James Clarke; *158* 30.12.1875, William Phillips, James McWalter & Henry Chambers (trading as Phillips, McWalter & Chambers: pl. 405); *172* 15.9.1876, Angus Maclean; *177* 9.3.1877, Joseph Turnell; *180* 4.8.1877, A. Maclean (see pls. 334, 361, 459).

(2) *191* 16.1.1878, A. Maclean; *208, 209* 27.3.1879, W. P. Denton; *266* 28.7.1880, A. Maclean (also New South Wales, pl. 329, no. 90); *309* 19.10.1882, *idem*; *241* 12.1.1880, *idem*.

(3) *268* 5.8.1880, A. Maclean (also New South Wales, pl. 329, no. 96); *333* 17.7.1884, *idem*; *338, 335, 336, 340, 337* 5.8.1884, J. Cochrane & G. C. Scott (see pls. 336, 391).

(4) *381* 14.6.1886, J. Cochrane & G. C. Scott; *360* 15.7.1885, J. Laughton; *366* 21.10.1885, M. Ratcliffe; *371, 372* 20.1.1886, W. K. Thomson & S. Renwick (trading as J. McEwan & Co.: see p. 55).

(5) *375* 8.3.1886, G. Waterstrom (trading as A. Maclean); *378, 379* 8.6.1886, C. Monteath & Sons; *383, 385* 14.6.1886, J. Cochrane & G. C. Scott; *405* 18.1.1887, *idem*.

334

333 A page from the large undated catalogue of Jenkins & Law's Birmingham Foundry, Melbourne. The same designs were registered in Victoria in 1870–73 by Lyster & Cooke. **334** Two plates of baluster panels from the beautifully engraved catalogue of William Stephens's Excelsior Foundry, Melbourne (see p. 9), 1901. The catalogue includes older designs, often registered by other firms, as Stephens was a wholesale merchant too (e.g. compare nos. 8 and 14 with pl. 331, nos. 4 and 1; and no. 11 with pl. 329, no. 32). For no. 6, see pl. 387.

South Australia designs (see pp. 52, 69–72)

335 Designs registered in 1880–85 (see note on pl. 329):

(1) *1* 4.3.1880, D. Garlick; *7* 17.11.1880, *idem*; *10* 7.7.1881, Forwood, Down & Co.; *20* 9.10.1882, D. Garlick.

(2) *21* 4.7.1883, Revell, Adams & Co. (pls. 337, 425); *22* 21.3.1883, D. Garlick; *23* 29.3.1883, W. F. de Mole & G. E. Farrar; *32* 1.9.1883, D. Garlick.

(3) *33* 9.9.1883, Revell, Adams & Co.; *35* 1.10.1883, J. W. Carr; *36* 24.10.1883, G. E. Fulton & Co. (see p. 70); *37* 11.12.1883, D. Garlick.

(4) all by G. E. Fulton & Co.: *39* 2.4.1883; *42* 15.7.1884; *43, 44* 16.7.1884.

(5) *47* 16.7.1884, G. E. Fulton & Co.; *48* 26.7.1884, J. Hill & A. G. Pearce (trading as Hill & Pearce); *49* 22.8.1884, D. Garlick & Son; *52* 27.2.1885, G. E. Fulton & Co.

No. 422.

No. 423.

No. 418A.
Sizes 2 ft. 4 in. and 3 ft. 1 in.

No. 425.

No. 416A.
Sizes 2 ft. 0 in., 2 ft. 3 in. and 2 ft. 8½ in.

No. 417A.
Sizes 2 ft. 2½ in., 2 ft. 9½ in. and 3 ft. 4¼ in.

No. 419A.
Sizes 2 ft. 3 in., 2 ft. 10⅞ in., and 3 ft. 3 in.

No. 420A.
Sizes 2 ft. 2 in. and 3 ft. 2⅞ in.

36

Plates from the catalogue of the 'Sun' Foundry of A. C. Harley & Co., Adelaide, 1914 (see p. 70).

336 'Brackets and Twin Brackets, with Frieze and Fringe combined'. Daisies are shown in nos. 422 (see pl. 427) and 418A, and fern fronds in no. 423 (pls. 332, 391). No. 420A also appears in New South Wales and Victoria (pls. 329, 332).
337 'Verandah and Balcony Railings'. For no. 565 see pls. 335 (no. 21) and 425; for no. 570, pl. 418. No. 567, also advertised by Macfarlane's and Watson, Gow & Co. of Glasgow (pl. 32), appears in Sydney and in Tasmania (pls. 362, 458).

No. 565.

No. 566.

No. 567.

No. 568.

No. 569.

No. 570.

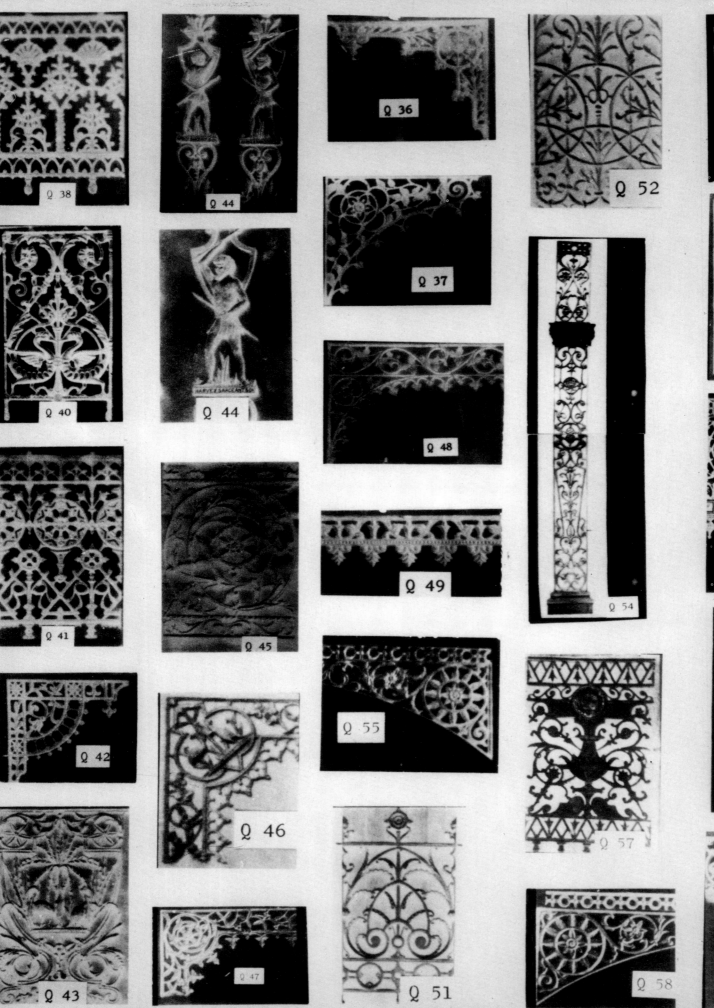

Q 38

Q 44

Q 36

Q 52

Q 40

Q 44

HARVEY&SARGEANT&Co

Q 37

Q 48

Q 41

Q 45

Q 49

Q 54

Q 42

Q 55

Q 46

Q 57

Q 43

Q 47

Q 51

Q 58

Q 61

Q 62

Q 63

Q 64

Q 65

339 A page from the early 20th-century catalogue of Metters Ltd, of Adelaide, Sydney and Perth. Curiously, several designs had Victoria registrations: no. 134 was registered in 1882 by A. Maclean and no. 142 (ferns in a 'rustic' frame) in 1884 by Cochrane & Scott (pl. 332); no. 144, symbolizing plenty and good fortune, was registered in 1892 by Cochrane & Scott, and appears in Melbourne (pl. 409).

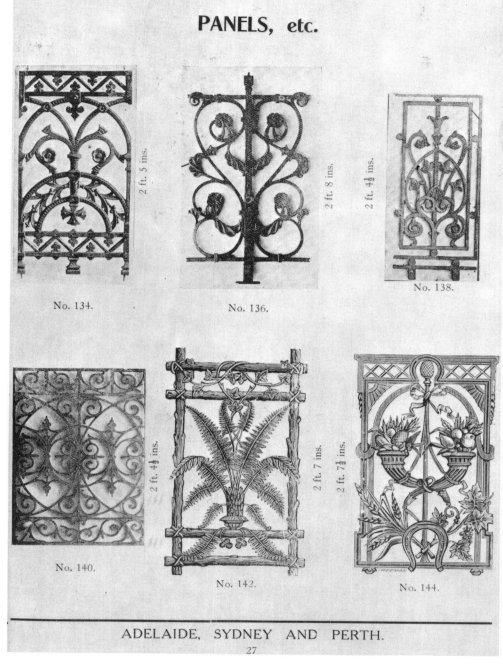

Queensland designs (see pp. 52, 72–74)

338 Designs registered in 1887–88 (see note on pl. 329)

(1) *38* 19.1.1887, A. Overend & Co. (compare pl. 356); *40* 4.3.1887, J. Crase & W. Wilson (registered in New South Wales in 1882: pl. 329); *41, 42* 21.4.1887, J. Crase; *43* 9.5.1887, Harvey Sargeant & Co. (see pls. 343, 455).
(2) *44–47* 9.5.1887, H. Sargeant & Co. (for 44 and 46, see pls. 342, 343, 455, and pp. 52–55).
(3) all by A. Overend & Co.: *36, 37* 19.1.1887; *48, 49* 13.5.1887; *55* 12.9.1887; *51* 16.6.1887.
(4) *52* 25.6.1887, A. Overend & Co.; *54* 12.9.1887, *idem*; *57* 3.8.1887, J. Crase; *58* 12.9.1887, A. Overend & Co.
(5) *61* 5.1.1888, A. Overend & Co. (pl. 442); *62* 13.1.1888, J. Crase; *63, 64* 20.1.1888, J. Hall & Son; *65* 14.2.1888, *idem*.

Indigenous Australian designs (see pp. 52–55)

340 The sulphur-crested cockatoo appears in this detail from a delicate frieze and bracket. It was registered in New South Wales in 1884 by D. & R. Bradford (no. 180).

341

341 A rare frieze and bracket featuring kookaburras, in profile and with outspread wings.
342, 343 A fascinating baluster panel and matching bracket showing aborigines, emus and kangaroos with some indigenous vegetation (see also pl. 455). For propriety the aborigines have been fitted with skirts of banana leaves. Proud of their creations (registered in Queensland in 1887 – pl. 338, nos. 43, 44, 46), Harvey Sargeant & Co. prominently displayed their name on the bracket. On the balustrade the Tudor rose, Scottish thistle, Irish shamrock and Welsh leek allude to Australians' origins.

342

343

344

345

346

Corio Villa, Geelong, Victoria (see pp. 60–63)

344 The villa, shown in *Illustrations of Iron Structures, for Home and Abroad,* by Charles D. Young & Co. of Edinburgh. In the house as built in 1856 (pl. 345), the bow shown at the far right was placed to balance the other by the front door, and the front veranda has square filigree rather than round columns. (Reproduced by courtesy of the Royal Institute of British Architects, London) **345** The villa itself, seen from a similar angle in 1875, before the portico (pl. 350) and late Victorian wing had been added. The two bows are hidden by conifers. **346** Above the portico (see pl. 350) is the family crest of Alfred Douglass, builder of the villa, supported by Scottish thistles. It was probably cast in Victoria, though it could have come from Scotland.

347   348

347, 348 Details of gable and veranda
facing north (left, in pl. 345).
Everything is iron – the finials,
bargeboards, rose window, parapet,
guttering and small lions' heads,
curved friezes of the arcades with large
lions' heads, and filigree capitals and
columns. 349 Balustrade on the 1890
addition to the villa – a pattern
designed in the 1820s by Henry Shaw
for Upper Woburn Place in London
(see pl. 12).

349

Corio Villa, Geelong (see pp. 60–63)

350 The north-western corner (at the left in pl. 345).
All is iron – walls and decoration. Between the two
bowed sun-porches is a portico with wooden
columns and a crest (pl. 346), added after 1875, but
using the same patterns. The veranda on the left,
originally open, had been enclosed *c*. 1890
(compare the balustrade with that in pl. 349); since
this picture was taken, it has been restored (pl. 348).
In front of each bow is one of the 'Medici Vases' (see
p. 63), illustrated by Cottingham in 1824 and made
by Young's of Edinburgh.

351

Sydney, New South Wales

The Rocks (see p. 66)

351 Gloucester Street, above Sydney Cove West, is shown in a 19th-century photograph by Norman Selfe. The two balconies are of the most common English patterns: for the Gothic design on the Ocean Wave Hotel see e.g. pl. 41; for the anthemion pattern on the Family Grocer see Cottingham's 1824 *Director* (above, pl. 3), and also, e.g., pls. 35 and 74. (Reproduced from the La Trobe Collection, State Library of Victoria)

352 Linsley Terrace on Lower Fort Street. (The Harbour Bridge may be glimpsed on the right.) The houses are unusually wide; unfortunately the balcony fronts have been filled in. The columns are marked 'J. R. Bubb, Victoria Foundry' (compare pl. 377). **353** Stair railing on No. 36 Loftus Street, between The Rocks and Woolloomooloo. **354, 355** Forbes Street, Woolloomooloo (see p. 66), in the early morning. How undistinguished No. 32 (pl. 355) would look without its ironwork! The pattern of the balustrade can be seen in Paris, at No. 144 Boulevard Haussmann.

Sydney

Glebe (see p. 67)

356 An unusual wedding-cake arrangement at Nos. 16 and 18 Mansfield Street, 1885. The balustrade pattern appears again at Fernleigh Castle (pl. 367), and resembles a Queensland registration (pl. 338).

357 Kerribree, now Camden College, of 1889, has a breakfront iron balcony. For the frieze and brackets see pls. 329 (no. 144) and 330 (no. 10).

358 A balconette at Talford and Marlborough Streets. The balustrade is a single-faced casting of a pattern registered in Victoria in 1872 by Cross & Laughton (and see p. 72), with the hollow side, oddly, facing out (compare pl. 455).

356

357

358

Paddington (see p. 67)

359, 360 Winding streets, following the tracks made by early vehicles to ease the steep rise from Port Jackson, add to the attractiveness of the area. Pl. 360 shows a recently preserved large corner house, transformed into a gallery of primitive art. The balustrade may be compared to pl. 329 (no. 32) and pl. 334 (no. 11); the frieze and bracket appear in the catalogue of Holdsworth MacPherson of Sydney (pl. 330, no. 13).

361

362

363

361 Wybalena, an unusual sandstone house with iron apron and cresting. The balustrade pattern was registered in Victoria in 1877 (see pl. 332, no. 180, pl. 334, no. 4, and pl. 438). **362** The back veranda of St Malo before demolition. For the balustrade pattern see pl. 337 (no. 567) and pl. 458. The Ionic columns came from Burdekin House in Macquarie Street. **363** No. 1 Madeline Street: the balustrade and snowflake-like brackets were registered by A. T. Rees & Co. in 1883 (pl. 329, nos. 132, 135). **364** Curved steps leading up to the veranda of Passy, built about 1854 by Italian stonemasons for the French Consul, M. Sentis. Note the cast iron boot-scraper in the form of a lyre.

365

Sydney

365 Domremy Presentation College, First Avenue, Five Dock. The deep layer of iron with a wide anthemion pattern below the veranda is quite uncommon. The lookout, or captain's walk, has a narrower anthemion pattern. **366, 367** Fernleigh Castle, Fernleigh Gardens, Rose Bay, in 'Scotch Baronial' or castellated style, has anachronistic balconies and porch of iron. Two lions guard the main entrance. The porch, a later addition, leads off to a raised veranda which affords a magnificent view of the harbour and its bridge. The balustrade pattern has already been seen in Glebe (pl. 356).

Sydney

368 The smallest house in Sydney – appropriately numbered 43½ Edgeware Road, Newtown. A porch with a pediment, a veranda, a balcony with an ogee roof, and a full complement of ironwork are packed into this tiny frontage. Coloured tiles are added for further decoration and sprigs of flowers adorn the walls. The balustrade pattern is shown in the catalogue of Holdsworth MacPherson of Sydney (pl. 331, no. 4).

369–371 An original mind produced unusual components for the veranda of the Lucy Gullett Nursing Home, Bexley. A *rinceau* grapevine frieze is supported by brackets with passion flowers and palm-frond-bearing winged female figures, while consoles with similar figures support the canopy. The curious columns have small curved shelves (pl. 371), probably designed to hold flowerpots.

369

370

371

372

373

375

Sydney

372 No. 2 Darley Street, Darlinghurst, has a very deep, encrusted frieze with a prominent fringe and sunflowers in the spandrels. 373 A very rare fox and grapes frieze, on a terrace since demolished. 374 Winged dragons form brackets on No. 198 Ernest Street, North Sydney. 375 Simpson's 'Vase Balcony Iron', using Adam features, registered in 1885. 376 Birds flanking a bowl of fruit, on the Aurora Restaurant. The pattern, advertised by Harley's of Adelaide (no. 966) and McDowall, Steven & Co. of Glasgow, appears in Beirut (pl. 505).

374

377 Elizabeth Farm House, Parramatta, the oldest house in Australia (1793), has later iron columns by Bubb & Son of Sydney (see pl. 352). **378** A typical column with elaborate filigree pattern and a flat capital, below a *rinceau* frieze. The column doubles as a support for the picket fence that borders the footpath. **379** Baluster panels sometimes replace spears or pickets in fences. **380** Hollow square gateposts at No. 360 Moore Park Road bear the maker's name and address: D. & R. Bradford, 323 Castlereagh Street, Sydney. More massive than usual, they have filigree work on two sides and arabesques of similar pattern on the alternate panels.

381

Melbourne, Victoria

National Trust houses

381, 382 Como, South Yarra, built in the 1850s before the great age of cast iron in Melbourne (see p. 69). The ironwork, imported from Scotland, is unique in resembling common iron fencing. Only the balustrade of the veranda (paved with white marble) has a decorative panel in the middle of each bay.

383, 385 Illawarra, Toorak, begun in 1889 (see p. 69). The ironwork designs have no parallels, and were probably made for the house. The frieze consists of deep wood-framed patterns, with spandrels and brackets to match, while the arch of the porch has a different pattern. On each side of the porch rounded balconies project, supported by five massive festooned brackets.

384 Rippon Lea, Hotham Street, Elsternwick (see p. 69). A large cast iron *porte-cochère*, visible on the right, was added in the 1880s. On the left is a vast iron fernery, through which a stream flows.

383

384

385

386

Melbourne

Parkville

386 The classic Melbourne apron, at No. 14 Fitzgibbon Street. The paired round columns have composite capitals and spandrels that match the brackets. The baluster pattern was registered in Victoria in 1888 by Maclean (no. 461). The hollow square gate piers, with central lions' heads and spherical tops, will often be seen again. **387, 389** One of Melbourne's many terraces, in which the roofs run from front to back (unlike Sydney, pl. 359). Sydenham Terrace in Gatehouse Street is an early, modest design: the only iron is the fences and balustrades, the latter with bold sunflowers characteristic of the Aesthetic Movement (see Stephens's catalogue: pl. 334, no. 6).
388 A staggered terrace on a curve in The Avenue.

387

388

389

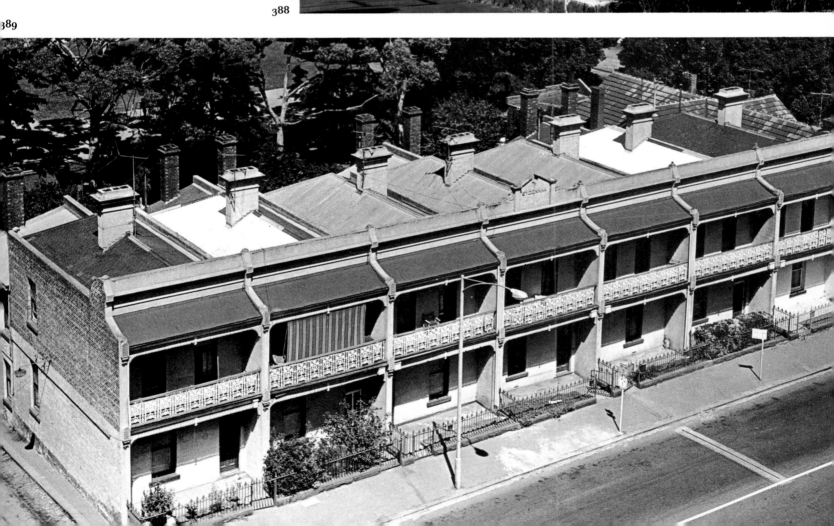

391

Melbourne

Parkville

390, 391 Looking out to the openwork porch of St Andrew's Hall, 190 The Avenue, and a detail of its fern-pattern ironwork, registered in 1884 by Cochrane & Scott (pl. 332, nos. 340, 337).
392, 393 Wardlow, an Italianate house of 1888 in Park Drive. The baluster pattern appears in the Queensland register for 1888 in the name of J. Crase (no. 74).

390

392

393

394

394, 395 Marmion and Rothsay, Morrah Street, are typical in their exuberant stucco ornamentation and have interesting 'Aesthetic' ironwork of ultimately Japanese inspiration, advertised by Stephens of Melbourne (see p. 53) and by Metters. In each panel at the left is a sunflower in an urn (compare pl. 387); the diagonal probably represents waves, while top right the life-giving sun shines down. Note the centre drop in the frieze.

395

396

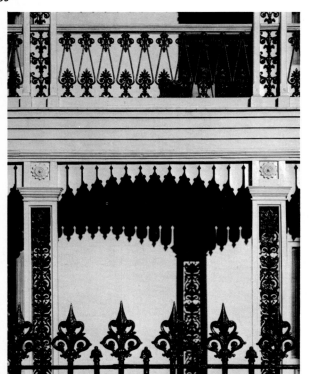

397

398

399

Melbourne

East Melbourne

396 Heavy stucco, iron gate piers, and a frieze with flowers (the other way up, in pl. 400) on No. 70 Albert Street. **397** Filigree columns unusually combined with wooden trimming, at the corner of Powlett and Gipps Streets. Note the openwork pickets of the fence. **398** Pairs of houses are common: Nos. 20 and 22 Morrison Place have paired columns (as pl. 386) and drops in the centre of the frieze. **399, 400** Tasma Terrace, Parliament Place, built in 1886 and later extended, and now used by the National Trust of Australia (Victoria). Stone walls are topped by fences and gates. Large brackets form complete arches. Compare the frieze with pl. 396, the lower balustrade with pls. 332 (no. 180, of 1877) and 334.

400

401

Melbourne   **401** Victoria Terrace in Simpson Street, East Melbourne, 1886; to the right a humble terrace of 1873.
402 No. 119 Drummond Street, Carlton, is one of the few surviving buildings with an open balcony.
The baluster pattern appears in the catalogue of McDowall, Steven & Co. of Glasgow. At first
imported, it was later cast in Australia, and advertised by Harley & Co. of Adelaide (no. 20).
403 St Edmonds Terrace, Drummond Street, Carlton, has a curved version of the balusters used
on Wardlow (pls. 392, 393).

402

403

404 No. 29 Sackville Street, Kew. The balusters are the same as in pl. 386. The lower frieze, unusually deep, consists of two variations on the same pattern. All the filigree elements of the veranda differ from those of the balcony. **405** The Parsonage, Richmond Hill, a breakfront with clustered columns and tracery-filled pediment (compare Brisbane, pls. 439, 443, and New Orleans, pl. 306). For the balustrade, see pl. 332.

406

408

407

Melbourne

406 A British Empire frieze (see p. 52, no. 3). **407** A matching Adamish set. Compared with a New South Wales registration in 1893 (nos. 352, 370) and a Sydney catalogue (pls. 330, 331), the frieze appears upside-down. **408** A design based on holly. **409** Balusters symbolic of plenty, registered in 1892 by Cochrane and Scott (no. 635; and see pl. 339).

409

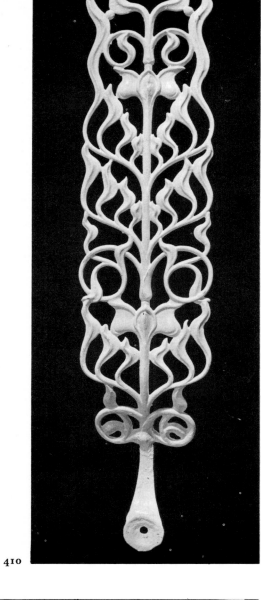

410

411

410 An Art Nouveau baluster. **411** Gate and overthrow of No. 997 Burke Road, Hawthorn, advertised by Macfarlane's of Glasgow and by Harley's and Fulton's of Adelaide, with slightly different measurements.

Melbourne

412 Cast iron crowns on the flamboyant Princess Theatre, Spring Street.

412

Melbourne

413 The gates of Benvenuta, Drummond Street, Carlton, include Renaissance masks.
414 Drinking fountain outside North Melbourne Post Office, an Australian copy of a popular design by Macfarlane's of Glasgow (p. 24).
415 Detail of the Eastern Market, founded in 1859 and tragically demolished in 1960. The arms of Melbourne bear a fleece, spouting whale, bull and ship.
416 Railings in the library of the Law Courts, built in 1875–84.

413

414   416

415

417

418

Adelaide, South Australia (see pp. 69–72)

417 Hindley Street, *c.* 1879. A shopping area showing a variety of verandas and balconies, some of which exist today. The verandas flush with the street, forming arcades (as in New Orleans, pls. 298–300), are features of the city's business district. In the left foreground an ornate lamp is fixed to a spandrel. The pattern of the balustrade above it is found also on the East End Market Hotel (pl. 418). **418** Balustrade of the East End Market Hotel, no. 570 in the catalogue of Harley's of Adelaide (pl. 337).

419–421 As elsewhere in Australia, hotels have been good preservers of cast iron. All the ironwork elements on the Eagle Hotel, 46 Hindley Street, probably built in 1867, appear in Harley's catalogue. The balustrade of the Kalgoorlie Hotel, 111 Hindley Street (pl. 420), appears in both Harley's and Fulton's catalogues; the frieze, and a variant on the bracket, in Harley's. The Botanic Hotel (pl. 421), at the corner of North and East Terraces (pp. 69–70), has a spectacular double recession and simple ironwork.

422 Queen's Chambers, 19 Pirie Street, built in 1869 as professional rooms by Garlick and McMinn.

423

Adelaide
(see pp. 69–70)

423, 426 Admaston, 219 Stanley Street, North Adelaide. Pl. 423 shows the rear view of the house; frieze, brackets and fringe appear in Harley's catalogue. In pl. 426 we are looking across the front fence (Harley's pattern no. 876) at the balustrade, featured in Harley's catalogue but also registered in Victoria in 1875 by Phillips, McWalter & Chambers (no. 158), and in New South Wales in 1881 (pl. 329, no. 89). **424** At No. 136 Jeffcott Street, North Adelaide, the balcony is recessed (compare pl. 421). Its pattern is that seen in pls. 423 and 426. The fence, typically on a stone base, is shown by Harley as a grave fence (no. 802). **425** No. 13 Norwood Parade. For the balustrade, registered in 1883, see pl. 335, no. 21. It and the capitals appear in Harley's catalogue. The brackets form an arch to support a wooden beam, and there are two patterns in each spandrel. **427** An unusual pavilion at No. 7 Prescott Terrace, a house of golden stone with stucco trim. The ironwork of daisy pattern is shown in several catalogues, for instance Harley's (pl. 336, no. 422), and Stephens's of Melbourne (see p. 53). Note the elaborate columns.

424

426

425

42

428

Adelaide (see p. 70)

428, 430 Birksgate, Glen Osmond, was a vast and
fascinating mansion profusely ornamented by delicate
cast iron, sadly demolished when its grounds were sold
for a housing estate. A central section of the veranda
projected, with paired columns like those of the
balcony above. Balcony, veranda and projection had
three different types of bracket. On either side there
were bow windows (pl. 430), serving as suntraps and
shelters from the wind. The castings at the top of each
bow were registered in Victoria in 1870 by William
Hutchison (no. 7).

429 Two fashionable pediments, one filled with iron
tracery, on a house with curious brackets and with iron
finial and cresting on the roof.

429

432

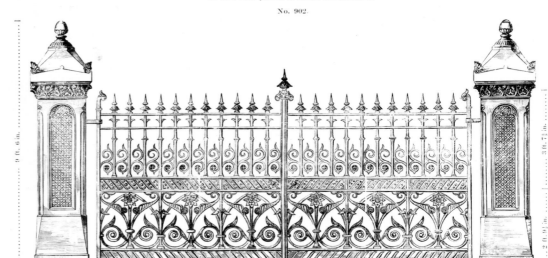

433

Adelaide

and Macfarlane's of Glasgow (see p. 70)

431-433 The piers of the Memorial Hospital, Sir Edwin Smith Avenue (pl. 431) appear in Macfarlane's catalogue (see pl. 27), but they are marked 'G. E. Fulton Ltd/Makers/Adelaide', and the design was advertised by both Harley's (pl. 433) and Fulton's. (We have already seen the fence, a Harley product, at Admaston, pl. 426.) The ironwork of No. 261 North Terrace (pl. 432), on the other hand, not only features in Macfarlane's catalogue but bears their trademark (pl. 27, and p. 24). Locally made copies of the piers also exist, and the fence is illustrated by both Macfarlane (no. 809) and Harley (no. 225). **434** Macfarlane's trademark, almost obliterated by paint, appears on the base of a column at No. 178 Stanley Street, North Adelaide. The unusually wide balustrade is not so marked; it is a copy of a variant Macfarlane design advertised by both Fulton's and Harley's (p. 72). **435, 436** Bandstand in Elder Park, shown in Macfarlane's catalogue (see pl. 24). The columns bear the Scottish firm's imprint in a small oval, and, near the base, the much larger inscription: 'Walter Macfarlane & Co., Saracen Foundry'.

437 Morphett Street railway footbridge, since demolished, with Holy Trinity Church, North Terrace, in the background. The balustrade combines simplified Gothic tracery with Greek anthemion.

435

436

434

437

Brisbane, Queensland (see pp. 72–74)

438 The Brisbane vernacular. This small house is raised on wooden stumps, capped by metal saucers, to deter white ants. Its veranda is roofed with corrugated iron and shaded by slatted blinds, while lattice-work panels and doors screen the open front door of the house from view. The baluster pattern (seen also in pl. 444) was registered in Victoria in 1877 (pl. 332, no. 180); and appears in the catalogue of Stephens of Melbourne (pl. 334, no. 4).
439 Beverley Wood, Jordan Terrace, Bowen Hills. An elegant portico with filigree columns gives the air of a Georgian breakfront house; its openwork pediment ventilates the roof (see also pls. 440, 448). The bases of the columns bear the name Smith, Forrester & Co. of Brisbane. The balustrade pattern was registered in Victoria in 1872 (no. 70), and appears in an Adelaide catalogue (see above, p. 72, no. 957). Both illustrations indicate that here it is upside-down. **440** Variations on the vernacular at No. 14 Sutherland Avenue, Ascot, with a very high latticed base and fanciful pavilion. The balustrades are of a simple columnar pattern common in Brisbane and are single-sided (see p. 74). The stair balusters are more ornate.

438

441

Brisbane (see pp. 72–74)

441 Massive curvaceous brackets support awnings to shade windows. This house, in Richmond Street, Morningside, is owned by the grandson of Enos Harvey, founder of Harvey's Foundry, later Harvey Sargeant & Co. (see pls. 338, 342, 343). **442** Fern (*Asplenium*) pinnules at No. 32 Whitehill Road, Eastern Heights, Ipswich: a pattern registered in 1888 by A. Overend & Co. (pl. 338, no. 61). **443** In Dean Street, Toowong, a portico is reached by a double flight of stairs, while a simpler double flight leads to the lower floor. The balusters are of two patterns, the wider ones incorporating Scottish thistles. **444** Brackets set at right angles support an overhanging balcony. The baluster pattern, seen already in Brisbane, also appears in Victoria and in South Australia (see the caption to pl. 438). **445, 446** The deep Queensland frieze appears in its dense, shade-giving form at the former Methodist Margaret Marr Home for Children (now belonging to the Education Department), where it is made up of three patterns. But the frieze of the Carlton Hotel, Queen Street, has such an open pattern that it gives little shade – as the shadow demonstrates. With its *rinceau* pattern it resembles the wide Queensland baluster panels (pl. 452) rather than a conventional frieze.

443

442

444

445

446

Brisbane (see pp. 72–74)

447, 448 The Bellevue Hotel at the corner of Alice and George Streets, a traditional lunching place for transit passengers on Orient and P & O liners. The magnificent ironwork comprises columns set at the edge of the pavement that support a curved roof and two tiers of recessed balconies. On the top floor is a small iron-filled pediment (compare pls. 439, 443). The balustrades figure in the catalogue of Macfarlane's of Glasgow (pl. 23). It seems likely that a Scottish specimen was used for repetitive casting in Brisbane, for the Macfarlane trademark is not to be found, and the castings are single-faced, rough, flat and hollowed out on the inner side (compare pl. 455).

449, 450 One of the outstanding buildings of
Brisbane is the magnificent Queensland Club,
founded in 1859. Columns of the pedimented
balcony above the entrance door bear the maker's
name, J. W. Sutton & Co. of Brisbane. Pl. 449 shows
one of the long wide balconies with massive
columns. The balusters are single-faced castings of a
design registered in Victoria in 1873 by Holland &
Hutchison (no. 110), similar to one in the catalogue
of Stephens of Melbourne (see above, p. 53, no. 16).
The main staircase of the club (pl. 450) has delicate
balusters with a dominant anthemion pattern.

451

453

Brisbane (see pp. 72–74)

451 The Customs House of 1887 has an unusual balustrade of double anthemion pattern (see also pls. 365, 453), which occasionally incorporates the initials VR for Victoria Regina. **452** A wide balustrade panel, common in Brisbane public buildings, in the General Post Office, 1872–76, cast by R. R. Smellie & Co. of Brisbane. **453** Double anthemion-patterned balustrade at No. 76 Yabba Street, Ascot, seen on the Customs House (pl. 451) and in Sydney (pl. 365). **454** Ecclesiastical Gothic – a very rare thing – befits a former convent in Cordelia Street, South Brisbane. **455** Back view of single-faced castings (see p. 74) at El Arish, 11 Gore Street, Albion. An exercise in Australiana registered in 1887 by Harvey Sargeant & Co. (pl. 338, nos. 43, 44, and pl. 343).

452

454

455

Tasmania (see p. 74)

456 The portico of Hythe, Wilmore's Lane, near Longford. In 1831 the architect Samuel Jackson asked the owner, Mr Weston, to order two very light sets of ironwork from England, and the balcony pattern seen here is of the type used by Nash in Regent's Park in London (pl. 40) and shown by Cottingham (pl. 2). Hythe was unfortunately demolished recently because of poor foundations. **457** Vaucluse, near the Midland Highway between Perth and Campbell Town, existed in 1838; it was later extended at the back (not seen here) and given a spacious veranda with paired columns. The balustrade pattern is shown in the catalogue of Harley's of Adelaide (no. 575). **458** This veranda at Deloraine has columns cast by P. N. Russell of Sydney. The matching balustrade, seen in Sydney (pl. 362), was advertised by the Adelaide firms of Fulton and Harley (nos. 182, 567: see pl. 337) and by Macfarlane's of Glasgow. Watson, Gow & Co. show the columns as well (see pl. 32).

457

456

Tasmania (see p. 74)

459 Tahara, Deloraine, a symmetrical house probably built in the 1870s, with veranda and open balcony. The balustrade pattern, frequently seen, was registered in Victoria in 1877 (pl. 332, no. 180). **460, 461** Wybra Hall, Midland Highway, Mangalore, built *c.* 1906, has wide angled verandas and a central 'Italian Villa' tower with iron finial. The ironwork is of uncommon design, and made more fascinating by the varied planes of ornamentation. **462** Drinking fountain in the City Gardens, Launceston, presented by the city children to commemorate Queen Victoria's Golden Jubilee, 1887, and erected at the Diamond Jubilee, 1897. It bears the mark of Macfarlane's of Glasgow. With owls above the columns inside (an optional extra for the canopy shown in pl. 26), it is of a type registered in 1860 and used throughout Britain and the Empire.

461

463

464

465

Christchurch, New Zealand (see p. 74)

463, 465 A brick terrace of loggia type, unusual for New Zealand, in Victoria Square. The ironwork (pl. 465) embodying the rose, thistle, shamrock and leek is a clear declaration of allegiance of a type seen in many cities with British affinities (pls. 406, 489). **464** One of the many cast iron bridges over the Avon, this one near the meeting of Rolleston Avenue and Armagh Street overlooks Christs College, the oldest school in Christchurch. **466** Part of the façade of the Royal Hotel, 24 Oxford Terrace. The filigree columns are notable.

466

Wellington, New Zealand (see p. 74)

467 A common style of house in Wellington, built of wood because of fear of earthquakes. A veranda with small iron brackets and frieze, leading to the recessed front door, overlaps the symmetrically placed bay windows which are capped by iron cresting. The fence is illustrated in the catalogues of Fulton's and Harley's of Adelaide (see p. 71).

467

Empires and influences

India

468 'Banking Premises, Madras . . . Interior Ornamental Ironwork Supplied by Walter Macfarlane & Co., Saracen Foundry, Glasgow'; from *Illustrated Examples of Macfarlane's Architectural Ironwork*. The flavour is Indian, but few of the motifs are. (By courtesy of the Public Library of New South Wales)

Bombay (see p. 75)

469–71 Bombay balconies. Pl. 469 shows five adjoining houses, each with three tiers of iron-balustraded balconies and a central pediment. The balconies are cantilevered, without street-level columns. In pl. 470 we see the single-storey, roofed corner balcony, with an end view of another balcony with a different balustrade above. The ironwork in pl. 471, of two patterns, appears almost too delicate to have survived, but its lightness would have lessened freight charges. As usual, the columns are of wood.

468

472

Bombay (see p. 76)

472, 473 Fences are often made of cast iron elements set above a solid base. The wide panels in pl. 472 are similar to two patterns illustrated by Macfarlane's of Glasgow without the curved pieces at the sides: one, registered in 1867, in the 5th edition of their catalogue (no. 201), and even more like, no. 201 in the 6th edition. The Anjuman Fire Temple (pl. 473), built in 1899, has suitably Persian-style stone columns, but the strong fence incorporating a lamp-post is of British design.

474 Ornamented bridges at varied angles connect buildings in a compound.

Bombay (see p. 76)

475-477 Masina Hospital, Victoria Road, built in 1880 as the residence of Sir David Sassoon. Pls. 475 and 476 show the gates, cast by the Coalbrookdale Company, which combine a design shown at the Great Exhibition of 1851 (pls. 60, 61) with lamp finials and the Sassoon arms in the centre (pl. 476). The arms appear again in a magnificent casting on the stairs (pl. 477), erected in 1897 before the visit of the Prince of Wales.

475

476

477

478 A cast iron durbar hall manufactured for export to India by Macfarlane's of Glasgow, proudly shown in *Illustrated Examples of Macfarlane's Architectural Ironwork*. The design, unlike that of their banking hall (pl. 468), is thoroughly Indian in inspiration – except for the iron and glass roof. (By courtesy of the Public Library of New South Wales)

479

Cape Town, South Africa (see p. 76)

479, 480 As in Australia, hotels are excellent preservers of ironwork. The balustrade of the White House Hotel, at Strand and Long Streets (pl. 479), is, surprisingly, of a Neo-classical anthemion design seen in balconies of the 1820s in London (pl. 12). The Princess Royal in Long Street (pl. 480) has more common Victorian ironwork, with the usual South African alternation of wide and narrow balusters for the balcony; particularly striking is the stilt-like extension of its columns as it descends the hill.

481, 482 Hiddingh Avenue, Gardens. The Model Villa at No. 4 (pl. 481) shows a pronounced Dutch influence, with which the iron frieze, brackets, column and balustrade, gate and fence fit in happily. A terrace in the avenue recalls Melbourne, but the balusters are narrower, the framing wood, and the bold frieze and brackets have a rather crude flat appearance.

480

481

482

Hamilton, Bermuda (see pp. 76–77)

483 Ardleigh, Church Street, is a long, low house with a veranda in the British colonial idiom. The balustrade, of delicate Regency type, is related to the highly popular anthemion pattern illustrated by Cottingham in 1824 (pl. 3, bottom right). **484** A lavish flowering of iron on a restaurant called Hoppin' John's, Front Street. Most of the ironwork was reproduced from New Orleans patterns, and shows the familiar grapevine (compare pls. 296, 297), but the large roundels in the frieze were cast using a table-top as model.

483

Toronto, Canada (see p. 77)

485 The most striking cast ironwork in the city is the fence of Osgoode Hall (now the Law Courts of Upper Canada), made by the St Lawrence Foundry and erected in 1860. The gates were specially designed to prevent cows from trespassing on the lawns of the Hall. On the overthrow, rose, thistle, shamrock and leek symbolize the United Kingdom; above them two beavers, representing Canada, support a regal crown.

Montreal (see p. 77)

486 One of a number of buildings in the city which in their stonework and in the arrangement of iron balconettes and window guards clearly reveal their French origins: No. 3685 Ontario Avenue.

486

487

488

489

Quebec (see p. 77)

487 The Séminaire de Québec, founded in 1880, has three balconies supported on full-depth brackets as well as iron columns. **488** A typical balcony set above a canted bow window at No. 68 Sainte-Ursule, with narrow garlanded balusters and geometrical frieze and brackets. **489, 490** A view from the Terrasse Dufferin towards the Château Frontenac Hotel, and a detail of the balustrade base which combines the Canadian maple leaf (left) with symbols of the United Kingdom.

Tahiti (see p. 77)

491 The veranda of the Archevêché de la Mission Catholique, *c.* 1860. The narrow balusters would be light for transport as cargo. **492** A grave in the Cimetière de l'Uranie. A cross is subtly worked into the design of each baluster, and there are two large iron crosses of a type found in Catholic cemeteries in Europe. The fence posts appear again at the Mission Catholique. The cost of transporting the small amount of iron needed for a grave would be reasonable; and it may be noted that the balusters here are single-faced (see p. 74), with the back, visible on the far side of the enclosure, hollowed out.

491

493

494

Mauritius (see p. 78)

493, 494 No. 5 Mère Barthélemy Street, Port Louis, resembles the cruder buildings of Columbia, California (pl. 328). Its scrolling balustrade pattern is shown in the catalogue of George Smith's Sun Foundry of Glasgow (no. 417).

495 The gates of the Pamplemousses Botanical Gardens are of a design that won first prize in the Great Exhibition of 1851. They were the gift of a M. Lienard, almost certainly the Parisian sculptor in wood who worked with the iron founders Barbezat & Cie. and others. **496** The ornate columns at No. 25 St George Street, Port Louis, are inscribed: 'Lienard 1802. Barbezat & Cie., Val d'Osne'. The balustrade is also French in design (compare pls. 154, 155).

496

497

498

Mexico City (see p. 78)

497–501 The Kiosco de la Alameda de Santa Maria, made in Spain for the Paris Exhibition of 1889 and later presented to Mexico, is a complete cast iron structure in Moorish style, covered by a glass and iron dome topped by an eagle grasping a snake – the Mexican national emblem. Several of the city's distinctive long iron park-benches can be glimpsed in pl. 497.

499

502

503

Mexico City (see p. 78)

502, 503 Two balcony balustrades, probably imported by a local firm from the Parisian founders Barbezat & Cie. (see pp. 33, 78), in whose catalogue they appear. An elegant house in Paseo de la Reforma has a rich Renaissance design with mermen, winged cupids, birds and squirrels (compare pl. 166). In a poorer quarter, we find the familiar interlace pattern (Barbezat's no. 107; and compare pls. 154, 192).

504 A pavilion at the San Angel Inn, Hacienda Goychocea.

504

505

Beirut, Lebanon

505, 506 Two houses show ironwork with connections as far afield as Australia and Scotland. The Ardati Building, Manara, has a balustrade with birds and vases seen in Sydney (pl. 376) and advertised by McDowall, Steven & Co. of Glasgow as well as Harley's of Adelaide (no. 966). The Tufenkjian House, in the Sursock Quarter, shows a stair rail made of balcony balusters, inadequately adjusted to the slope. A similar design appears in the catalogue of Watson, Gow & Co. of Glasgow (see pl. 31).

506

Glossary

acanthus   A very common decorative motif based upon the leaf of the Greek Acanthus *Spinosus*, which has more pointed laterals than the rounded Roman type.

anthemion   From the Greek *anthos*, meaning flower. A common Greek and Roman motif resembling honeysuckle flowers, with symmetrically placed inward- or outward-curving petals rounded at the tip. A favourite motif for cast iron ornament.

apron   This word is used for convenience to designate the ornamental cast iron of balcony and veranda—which is added to, but not an essential part of, a building, just as an apron may be put on to cover the front of a person.

architrave   A moulding framing a doorway or window. In classical architecture, the lowest part of the entablature supported by columns.

Art Nouveau   A style which enjoyed a brief popularity *c.* 1890–1905, characterized chiefly by undulating or flame-like patterns.

balconette   A small balcony, usually for a single window.

balcony   A platform protruding from the face of a building above the ground floor, entered via doors, French windows or deep sash windows. The front is protected by a railing. It may be supported by brackets, columns or a veranda, or it may be cantilevered out from the wall. It may or may not have a roof, the latter type being designated in this text as an 'open balcony'.

baluster   A short vertical member of a series supporting the railing of a balcony, veranda, stair, or the upper part of an entablature. May be broad and panel-like.

balustrade   A row of balusters, or a single wide panel serving as guard on a balcony or landing.

caryatid   A sculptural female figure used instead of a column to support an entablature.

chamfer   A symmetrical bevel cutting off a corner. The term is commonly used in woodwork: it is used here for the corner of a building so treated.

console   An S-shaped bracket, with the smaller volute below.

coping   A projecting cap on top of a wall.

cornice   A projecting horizontal feature which crowns a façade (in classical architecture, the upper layer of the entablature).

entablature   In classical architecture, the three horizontal top members (cornice, frieze and architrave) that are supported by columns (of Ionic, Doric or Corinthian type). In Australia a house or terrace is often given a name which is cast on an oblong or curved upward projection of the entablature.

fanlight   A glazed semicircular or (applied loosely) rectangular panel fitting into a corresponding opening above a door, so called because of the frequent fan-like arrangement of the glazing bars.

filigree pillars or columns   Flat supporting panels of cast iron with a shallow open-work pattern, set in a framework of tall solid bars.

freestone   Easily-worked sandstone or limestone.

gallery   A roofed balcony, or, particularly in New Orleans, a covered veranda with balconies atop, the thin supporting pillars being set at the outer edge of the footpath.

lintel   A strong horizontal member above a door or window to carry the weight of the wall above.

loggia   A pillared wide veranda or balcony open on one or more sides.

newel post   A post supporting the handrailing at the foot or end of a stair.

open balcony   A balcony without a roof.

oriel window   A several-sided window protruding from the wall of an upper storey.

palmette   An ornament like a palm leaf, in the form of a flat radiating cluster with pointed tips, emanating from a stem or collar of leaves.

patera   A small circular or oval decoration in relief on a plain surface. A stylized flat Tudor rose is a common form.

pediment   A triangular low-pitched gable above a portico, door, window or entablature, or the decorated front of a gable.

piazza   A wide balcony, loggia or gallery with strong columns. In Charleston, South Carolina, it incorporates the main entrance to the house.

pilaster   A tall shallow rectangular projection attached to a wall, resembling a flattened column and having a capital.

porte-cochère   In France, tall double doors large enough for a wheeled vehicle to enter (though not necessarily intended for vehicles). In English usage, a porch allowing vehicles to draw up to the front door under shelter.

portico   An extended porch: a paved area along the entrance front of a building, with a roof – and in classical architecture a pediment – supported by columns.

repoussé work Wrought iron (or another metal) hammered out from the reverse side to form a design in relief.

rinceau A regular wavy branch or stem, of uniform width, from which spring, at regular intervals, subsidiary curling stems with foliage above and below the undulations of the main stem.

spandrel A narrow casting used between paired columns to continue the line of the balustrade or frieze and brackets.

stoep In the Netherlands, a veranda, or a platform in front of the entrance door approached by a flight of steps.

stoop A common term in the USA, derived from the Dutch word *stoep*, indicating a platform or porch reached by steps at the entrance to a building.

storeys All the parts of a house subdivided horizontally by floors. In English usage (followed in this book) the first storey is called the ground floor, the second storey the first floor and so on. In the USA the ground floor is called the first floor, and so on.

terrace A row of abutting houses of uniform style. Also, in Adelaide, Australia, an important wide street.

veranda A platform, often raised above ground level, with a roof supported by columns or pillars. Frequently confined to the front of the house, it may continue round the sides or even surround the house. Balconies may be super-imposed. In the USA, usually called a porch.

Bibliography

General

EVANS, JOAN. *Style in Ornament*, London, Oxford University Press, 1950.

GLOAG, JOHN and BRIDGWATER, DEREK. *A History of Cast Iron in Architecture*, London, George Allen and Unwin, 1948.

WEINREB & BREMAN LTD. *The Use of Iron in Construction and Decoration, with a supplement of trade catalogues from foundries and ironmongers* (Architecture, Catalogue 20), London, the authors, 1967. An invaluable work (though the Macfarlane catalogues are dated incorrectly).

Catalogues

The following is a selection from the catalogues consulted by the authors. The location of a firm's main office is given first; where a catalogue indicates branch offices or works, these are given in brackets. Since the catalogues are rare, the location of a copy is given whenever possible. The following abbreviations are used: BM British Museum, London; LC Library of Congress, Washington, D.C.; LNSW Library of New South Wales, Sydney; Met. Metropolitan Museum of Art, New York; V & A Victoria and Albert Museum, London.

BADGER, DANIEL D.: Architectural Iron Works of the City of New York, New York. *Illustrations of Iron Architecture, Made by the Architectural Iron Works of the City of New York*, 1865 (reprinted: see below, 'The United States', under Sturges). (Copy: LC.)

BARBEZAT & CIE., Paris, dated 1858 but including plates dated 1860 and 1861. (Copies: LC; the authors.)

BARTLETT, ROBBINS & Co., Baltimore, Md, n.d. [1866 or after]. For an earlier catalogue see Hayward, Bartlett & Co. (Copy: Enoch Pratt Free Library, Baltimore.)

BUNNETT & Co., London (Birmingham, Leeds, Liverpool, Glasgow, Melbourne and Cape Town), n.d. (Copy: the authors.)

CARRON COMPANY, Carron, Stirlingshire (Glasgow, Liverpool and London), 1891. (Copy: the authors.)

CHASE BROTHERS AND Co., Boston. *The Illustrated Catalogue of Iron Work*, 1859. (Copy: Met.)

COALBROOKDALE COMPANY (spelt Coalbrook-Dale), Coalbrookdale, Salop (Wellington, Salop, Bristol, London, Liverpool, Manchester, etc.). *Catalogue of Castings and Works in Metal*, 1875. (Copy: the authors.)

FISKE, J. W., New York. *Illustrated Catalogue of Iron Railings*, n.d. (Copy: Met.)

FULTON, G. E., & Co., Adelaide. *Illustrated Catalogue of Fulton's Castings*, 2nd ed., 1887. (Copy: South Australian Collection, State Library of South Australia.)

HARLEY, A. C., & Co., 'SUN' FOUNDRY, Adelaide. *'Sun' Foundry, Illustrated Catalogue*, 2nd ed., 1914. (Copy: the authors.) For the 1st ed. see Stewart & Harley.

HAYWARD, BARTLETT & Co., Baltimore, Md, n.d. [before 1866, when the firm became Bartlett, Robbins & Co.: see above]. (Copy: Enoch Pratt Free Library, Baltimore.)

HEMMING'S PORTABLE BUILDING MANUFACTORY, Bedminster, Bristol. *Hemming's Patent Improved Portable Houses*, n.d. [1853?] (Copy: Baillieu Library, University of Melbourne.)

HINDERER'S IRON WORKS, New Orleans, La. *A.I.A. File Data from Hinderer's Iron Works*, n.d. (Copy: the authors.)

—— *Cast Iron Lace Work*, n.d. (Copy: the authors.)

—— *Catalogue of Lawn Requisites*, n.d. (Copy: the authors.)

—— *Fountain Catalogue*, n.d. (Copy: the authors.)

—— *Garden and Lawn Requisites*, Catalog 39, 1931. (Copy: the authors.)

—— *Ornamental Iron Vases*, n.d. (Copy: the authors.)

HOLDSWORTH MACPHERSON, Sydney. n.d. (Present whereabouts unknown.)

JENKINS & LAW, BIRMINGHAM WORKS, Melbourne. n.d. (Copy: the authors.)

LAIDLAW, R., & SON, Glasgow (Edinburgh and London). *Pattern Book*, n.d. (Copy: the authors.)

LORIO IRON WORKS, New Orleans, La. *Catalog of Ornamental Ironwork*, 48th anniversary ed., 1954. (Copy: the authors.)

MACFARLANE, WALTER, & Co., SARACEN FOUNDRY, Glasgow (London). *Catalogue of Macfarlane's Cast Iron Manufactures*, 4th ed., n.d. [BM date 1862, though individual illustrations show later dates]. (Copy: V & A.)

—— *Catalogue of Macfarlane's Castings*, 5th ed., n.d. [BM date 1870/71]. (Copies: BM; LC; the authors.)

—— *Examples Book of Macfarlane's Castings*, n.d. [BM date 1876]. (Copies: BM; LC; the authors.)

—— *Illustrated Catalogue of Macfarlane's Castings*, 6th ed., n.d. [BM dates vol. I 1882, vol. II 1883]. This catalogue exists in at least three different sizes – the largest with large lithographic plates, the two smaller with engraved plates. (Copies: BM; LC; LNSW; the authors.)

—— *Illustrated Examples of Macfarlane's Architectural Ironwork*, n.d. [*c.* 1912]. (Copies: LNSW; Royal Institute of British Architects, London.)

MCDOWALL, STEVEN & Co., MILTON IRON WORKS, Glasgow (London). *Architectural & General Iron Castings*, 21st ed., sect. III, n.d. (Copy: the authors. A copy of the 20th ed. was acquired by the V & A in 1885.)

METTERS LTD, North Adelaide, Sydney and Perth, n.d. [*c.* 1900?]. (Copy: the authors.)

MOTT, J. L., IRON WORKS, New York (Chicago, Boston and San Francisco). *Catálogo Ilustrado*, 1883. (Copies: LC; Met.; the authors.)

—— '*M*' *Illustrated Catalogue and Price List of Statuary and Animals*, 1890. (Copies: LC; Met.; the authors.)

—— *Illustrated Catalogue* '*N*' *Entrance Gates, Railings, &c.*, 1891. (Copies: LC; Met.; the authors.)

—— *Illustrated Catalogue* '*Q*' *and Price List. Vanes, Bannerets, Finials, &c.*, 1892. (Copies: LC; Met.; the authors.)

—— *Examples of Metal Work*, 1895. (Copies: Met.; the authors.)

—— *Steam Boilers, Hot Water Heaters, Radiators*, 1900. (Copies: Met.; the authors.)

NEW YORK WIRE RAILING COMPANY, New York. *Iron Manufactures of the New York Wire Railing Company*, 1857. (Copies: LC; Met.) See also Wickersham.

RITCHIE, ALEXANDER & Co., London (Glasgow, Falkirk and Rotherham). *Architectural Iron Work*, 1904. (Copy: the authors.)

SMITH, GEORGE, & Co, SUN FOUNDRY, Glasgow (London and Dublin). *Catalogue of Architectural and Ornamental Castings*, n.d. (Copy: the authors.)

STEPHENS, WILLIAM, EXCELSIOR FOUNDRY, South Melbourne. *Illustrated Catalogue*, 1901. (Copy: School of Architecture Library, University of Melbourne. The original copper plates are in the authors' possession.)

STEVEN BROS. & Co., see McDowall, Steven & Co.

STEWART & HARLEY, 'SUN' FOUNDRY, Adelaide. '*Sun*' *Foundry, Illustrated Catalogue*, 1st ed., 1897. (Copy: South Australian Collection, State Library of South Australia.) For the 2nd ed. see A. C. Harley & Co.

WATSON, GOW & Co., ETNA FOUNDRY, Glasgow. (Copy: the authors. The BM possesses a different catalogue, deposited in 1881.)

WESTERVELT, A. B. & W. T., New York. *Cast and Wrought Iron Finials, Bannerets and Crosses*. (Copy: Met.)

WICKERSHAM, JOHN B., New York. *New York Wire Railing Works*, n. d. (Copy: Met.)

YOUNG, CHARLES D., & Co., Edinburgh (London, Liverpool and Glasgow). *A Short Treatise on the System of Wire Fencing, Gates, Etc. . . .* to which is appended an *Illustrated and Descriptive Catalogue of Ornamental Cast and Wrought Iron and Wire Work*, 1850. (Copy: the authors.)

—— *Illustrations of Iron Structures, for Home and Abroad*, n.d. [*c*. 1855]. (Copy: Royal Institute of British Architects, London.)

The British Isles

ADAM, ROBERT and JAMES. *The Works in Architecture of Robert and James Adam, Esquires*, London, the authors, vol. I 1773, vol. II 1779 (illustrated in Harris: see below).

BEGG, IAN and DENVER, BOYD. *Edinburgh, the New Town*, Edinburgh, Howie, 1967.

BOTTOMLEY, JOSEPH. *A Book of Designs*, London, 1793 (illustrated in Harris: see below).

BUNNETT & Co., London. See above, 'Catalogues'.

CARRON COMPANY, Carron, Stirlingshire. See above, 'Catalogues'.

—— *The Story of Carron Company*, Carron, Stirlingshire, n.d. [1959].

CHATWIN, AMINA. *Cheltenham's Ornamental Ironwork*, Cheltenham, Glos., the author, 1975. A copy was received after the present work was complete, but it must be included here as an admirable example of the combination of the history of the town and its wrought and cast iron manufacturers and manufactures, ranging from balusters to gas and electric light fittings. It also contains an interesting discussion of the 'heart and honeysuckle' pattern (see above, pl. 2, bottom right).

Coalbrookdale Company, Coalbrookdale, Shropshire. See above, 'Catalogues'.

Cottingham, Lewis Nockalls. *The Smith and Founder's Director*, London, the author, 1824 (illustrated in Harris: see below). A reprint of *The Ornamental Metal Workers' Director* (London, the author, 1823), with 22 additional plates. This book is so important that the description from the catalogue of Weinreb & Breman (see above, 'General') should be quoted: 'Second enlarged edition of this influential pattern book for a rapidly growing industry. First published eight months earlier, in October 1823, as the "Ornamental metal worker's director", the book contains examples of existing work, mainly in the London of Nash's days: Cumberland gates, Vintner's Hall (1822), Nash's own residence in Waterloo place. There is also a fine series of gas lights, on plates 37 to 44, and hundreds of examples of rosettes and small Roman and Gothic ornament "from drawings & casts in the author's possession" . . . Folio. Litho title, one leaf of printed text, and 82 litho plates printed by Hullmandel.'

—— Original pen and wash drawings for decorative cast iron work, *c.* 1820–40, bound in one volume. In the authors' possession. Described by Weinreb & Breman as a 'well-preserved collection, including a particularly fine series of 39 highly decorative designs for staircases and bannisters (some with lanterns): full-page plates, all in delicate colouring . . . throughout the book only one side of the paper has been used. The other drawings consist of four full-page verandahs, three coloured balustrade designs (on one leaf) and a group of 34 pen studies for ornamental gates and fences (on eighteen leaves). Measurements are included in each plate, some have price notations, and a few bear notes on execution for specific patrons: Manchester Bank, Mr Balfour Grosvenor Square, Lord Dovers White Hall, Mr Atkinson.'

Davis, Terence. *The Architecture of John Nash*, London, Studio, 1960.

Edinburgh Architectural Association. *Edinburgh: An Architectural Guide*, 1969.

Gibbs, James. *A Book of Architecture*, London, 1728 (illustrated in Harris: see below).

Harris, John. *English Decorative Ironwork from Contemporary Source Books, 1610–1836*, London, Tiranti, 1960. 168 illustrations including ironwork on buildings and from works by Inigo Jones, Tijou, Gibbs, Batty Langley, Isaac Ware, Robert and James Adam, J. Bottomley, I. and J. Taylor, Cottingham, Basevi, and Henry Shaw.

King, William Boughton. *King's Treatise on the Science and Practice of the Manufacture and Distribution of Coal Gas*, ed. T. Newbigging and W. T. Fewtrell, London, 1878–82.

Laidlaw, R., & Son, Glasgow. See above, 'Catalogues'.

Langley, Batty. *Ancient Masonry both in the Theory and in the Practice*, London, 1736 (illustrated in Harris: see above).

Le Clerc, Sebastien. *A Treatise of Architecture with Remarks and Observations*, London, 1723–24 (illustrated in Harris: see above).

Lindsay, John S. *An Anatomy of English Wrought Iron, 1000–1800*, London, Tiranti, 1964.

Lister, Raymond. *Decorative Cast Ironwork in Great Britain*, London, G. Bell and Sons, 1960.

McDowall, Steven & Co., Milton Iron Works, Glasgow. See above, 'Catalogues'.

MacFarlane, Walter, & Co., Saracen Foundry, Glasgow. See above, 'Catalogues'.

Musgrave, Clifford. *The Royal Pavilion, Brighton,* County Borough of Brighton, 1960.

Ritchie, Alexander & Co., London. See above, 'Catalogues'.

Roberts, Henry D. *A History of the Royal Pavilion Brighton with an Account of its Original Furniture and Decoration,* London, Country Life, 1939.

Ruskin, John. *The Seven Lamps of Architecture,* London, Smith, Elder & Co., 1849.

Shaw, Henry. *Examples of Ornamental Metal Work,* London, Wm. Pickering, 1836 (illustrated in Harris: see above).

Smith, George, & Co., Sun Foundry, Glasgow. See above, 'Catalogues'.

Steven Bros. & Co., see McDowall, Steven & Co.

Stroud, Dorothy. *The Thurloe Estate South Kensington,* London, Country Life for Thurloe Estates, 1959.

Summerson, John. *Georgian London,* London, Pleiades Books, 1945; rev. ed. Harmondsworth, Penguin Books, 1962.

—— *John Nash, Architect to King George IV,* London, G. Allen and Unwin, 1935.

Taylor, I. and J. *Ornamental Iron Work, or Designs in the Present Taste, for Fan-Lights, Stair-case-railing, Window-guard-irons, Lamp-irons, Palisades, & Gates,* London, the authors, n.d. [*c.* 1795] (illustrated in Harris: see above).

Tijou, Jean. *A New Booke of Drawings,* London, 1693 (illustrated in Harris: see above).

Ware, Isaac. *A Complete Body of Architecture,* London, 1756 (illustrated in Harris: see above).

Watson, Gow & Co., Etna Foundry, Glasgow. See above, 'Catalogues'.

Young, Charles D. *A Short Treatise on the System of Wire Fencing, Gates, Etc. as manufactured by Charles D. Young and Company,* bound with the *Illustrated and Descriptive Catalogue . . .,* Edinburgh, 1850 (see above, 'Catalogues').

Youngson, A. J. *The Making of Classical Edinburgh, 1750–1840,* Edinburgh University Press, 1966.

The Continent of Europe

Barbezat & Cie., Paris. See above, 'Catalogues'.

Doroshinskaya, Yelena and Kruchina, Vadim. *Leningrad, Guidebook,* Moscow, Novosti, n.d. [1969?].

Gosling, Nigel. *Leningrad,* London, Studio Vista, 1965.

Havard, Henry. *Dictionnaire de l'ameublement et de la décoration, depuis le XIIIe siècle jusqu'à nos jours,* Paris, Quantin, 1894.

Kolesova, O. *'With iron-tracings richly wrought . . .',* Leningrad, Aurora, 1970.

The United States

Badger, Daniel D. *Illustrations of Iron Architecture, Made by the Architectural Iron Works of the City of New York,* New York, 1865 (reprinted: see below, Sturges).

Bartlett, Robbins & Co., Baltimore, Md. See above, 'Catalogues'.

Bogardus, James. *Cast Iron Buildings: Their Construction and Advantages,* New York, 1856 (reprinted: see below, Sturges).

BORDEWICH, FERGUS M. 'New York's Largest Outdoor Museum, Made of Cast Iron', *The New York Times*, 23 February 1975.

BUNTING, BAINBRIDGE. *Houses of Boston's Back Bay: an Architectural History, 1840–1917*, Cambridge, Mass., Belknap Press of Harvard University, 1967.

CHASE BROTHERS AND CO., Boston. See above, 'Catalogues'.

Columbia Historic State Park, guide published by the Department of National Resources, Calif., n.d.

FISKE, J. W., New York. See above, 'Catalogues'.

GAYLE, MARGOT. 'Cast-Iron Architecture. The Victorian Prefab', *Americana*, January 1974.

—— and GILLON, EDMUND V., JR. *Cast-Iron Architecture in New York*, New York, Dover, 1974.

GREELEY, HORACE, et al. *Great Industries of the United States, being an Historical Summary of the Origin, Growth, and Perfection of the Chief Industrial Arts of this Country*, Hartford, Conn., J. B. Burr and Hyde, 1872.

HAYWARD, BARTLETT & Co., Baltimore, Md. See above, 'Catalogues'.

HINDERER'S IRON WORKS, New Orleans, La. *A.I.A. File Data from Hinderer's Iron Works*, New Orleans, La., n.d. And see above, 'Catalogues'.

JUNIOR LEAGUE OF SAN FRANCISCO, INC. *Here Today, San Francisco's Architectural Heritage*, San Francisco, Calif., Chronicle Books, 1973.

LATROBE, FERDINAND C. *Iron Men and their Dogs*, Baltimore, Md, Ivan R. Drechsler, 1941.

LORIO IRON WORKS, New Orleans, La. See above, 'Catalogues'.

LYNN, STUART M. *New Orleans*, New York, Bonanza Books, 1949.

MASSON, A. M. and OWEN, L. J. *Cast Iron and the Crescent City*, New Orleans, La., Gallier House, 1975. This booklet came out too late for full use to be made of it. It is illustrated, and contains lists of New Orleans foundries and a bibliography.

MOTT, J. L., IRON WORKS, New York. See above, 'Catalogues'.

NEW YORK WIRE RAILING COMPANY, New York. See above, 'Catalogues'.

ROMAINE, LAWRENCE B. *A Guide to American Trade Catalogues, 1744–1900*, New York, R. R. Bowker, 1960.

SAMUEL, MARTHA and RAY. *The Great Days of the Garden District and the Old City of Lafayette*, New Orleans, La., Parents' League of the Louise S. McGehee School, 1961.

Saugus Ironworks Restoration, American Iron and Steel Institute, 1957.

SHERBORN, DEREK. 'A New Face for Philadelphia', *Country Life*, CXLII, no. 3672, 20 July 1967, pp. 155–61.

SIMPSON, BRUCE L. *Development of the Metal Castings Industry*, Chicago, Ill., American Foundrymen's Association, 1948.

Specifications of Work and Particulars of Materials Required to be used in the Erection of Proposed Additions to the Peabody Institute, Baltimore, Md., Baltimore, Md, William K. Boyle and Son, 1875.

STONEY, SAMUEL GAILLARD. *This is Charleston, a Survey of the Architectural Heritage of a Unique American City*, rev. ed., Charleston, S.C., Carolina Art Association, 1960.

STURGES, WALTER KNIGHT, ed. *The Origins of Cast Iron Architecture in America* (reprint of publications by Badger and Bogardus: see above), New York, Da Capo Press, 1970.

WESTERVELT, A. B. & W. T., New York. See above, 'Catalogues'.

WESTON, OTHETO. *Mother Lode Album*, Stanford, Calif., Stanford University Press, 1948.

WHITEHILL, WALTER MUIR. *Boston: a Topographical History*, Cambridge, Mass., Belknap Press of Harvard University, 1959, 2nd ed., enlarged, 1968.

WICKERSHAM, JOHN B., NEW YORK WIRE RAILING WORKS. See above, 'Catalogues'.

WILSON, SAMUEL JR. *A Guide to Architecture of New Orleans – 1699–1959*, New York, Reinhold, 1959.

Australia and New Zealand

ALLEN, DAVID ELLISTON. *The Victorian Fern Craze*, London, Hutchinson, 1969.

ARCHITECTURAL PUBLICATIONS SOCIETY, LONDON. *Dictionary of Architecture*, London, Thomas Richards, n.d. [1853–92].

Australian Encyclopaedia, 3rd ed., Sydney, Angus and Robertson, 1927.

BUNNETT & Co., London and Melbourne. See above, 'Catalogues'.

CILENTO, R. and LACK, C. *Triumph in the Tropics: an Historical Sketch of Queensland*, Brisbane, Smith and Paterson, 1959.

COOMBE, E. H. *History of Gawler, 1837–1903*, Adelaide, Vardon and Sons, 1910.

'Coppin's Royal Olympic Theatre', *The Australian Builder and Land Advertiser*, no. 3, 16 August 1855, pp. 23–24.

'Drinking Fountains for the City', *The Australian Town and Country Journal*, II, no. 27, 9 July 1870, p. 6.

Fourteen Views of Old Adelaide. Sketches in 1840–49 by S. T. Gill, F. R. Nixon, S. Calvert and O. Korn, Adelaide, E. S. Wigg and Son, n.d. [c. 1889].

FOWLES, JOSEPH. *Sydney in 1848*, Sydney, the author, n.d. [c. 1849–50].

FULTON, G. E., & Co., Adelaide. See above, 'Catalogues'.

GEORGE, HEATHER. 'The Stately Homes of Hunter's Hill', *Walkabout*, XXIV, no. 9, 1 October 1958, pp. 27–28.

GOODMAN, GEORGE. *The Church in Victoria during the Episcopate of the Right Reverend Charles Perry*, Melbourne, Melville, Mullen and Slade, 1892.

HARLEY, A. C., & Co., 'SUN' FOUNDRY, Adelaide. See above, 'Catalogues'.

HEMMING'S PORTABLE BUILDING MANUFACTORY, Bedminster, Bristol, England. See above, 'Catalogues'.

HENN, L., AND Co. *A Series of Views of South Australia*, Adelaide, n.d. [c. 1879].

HERBERT, GILBERT. *Manning's Portable Colonial Cottages*, manuscript, 1974.

Historical Records of Australia, Sydney, Library Committee of the Commonwealth Parliament, 1914–25.

Historic Houses of Australia, North Melbourne, Victoria, Cassell Australia for the Australian Council of National Trusts, 1974.

HOLDSWORTH MACPHERSON, Sydney. See above, 'Catalogues'.

'Iron Church in Melbourne', *The Argus*, no. 1976, 3 September 1853.

JENKINS AND LAW, BIRMINGHAM WORKS, Melbourne. See above, 'Catalogues'.

KEEP, EDWARD. 'Some Reminiscences of my Life', *The Australasian Ironmonger, Engineer and Metal Worker*, XIV, no. 11, 1 November 1899, pp. 409–10.

LOUDON, J. C. *An Encyclopaedia of Cottage, Farm, and Villa Architecture and Furniture*, London, Longman, 1833.

LOYAU, G. E. *The Gawler Handbook*, Adelaide, Goodfellow and Hele, 1880.

McCoy, E. J. and Blackman, J. G. *Victorian City of New Zealand: Photographs of the Earlier Buildings of Dunedin*, Dunedin, John McIndoe, 1968.

Metters Ltd, North Adelaide, Sydney and Perth. See above, 'Catalogues'.

Morgan, E. J. R. and Gilbert, S. H. *Early Adelaide Architecture 1836 to 1886*, Melbourne, Oxford University Press, 1969.

Newell, P. and White, U. *Brisbane Sketch Book*, Adelaide, Rigby, 1967.

'Portable Iron Church for the Diocese of Melbourne', *The Illustrated London News*, XXII, no. 619, 30 April 1853, p. 324.

Robertson, E. Graeme. *Victorian Heritage; Ornamental Cast Iron in Architecture*, Melbourne, Georgian House, 1960; paperbound ed. Ure Smith, in association with Georgian House and National Trust of Australia (N.S.W., Victoria), 1974.

—— *Sydney Lace; Ornamental Cast Iron in Architecture in Sydney*, Melbourne, Georgian House, 1962.

—— *Ornamental Cast Iron in Melbourne*, Melbourne, Georgian House, 1967, and London, Routledge and Kegan Paul, 1972.

—— *Early Buildings of Southern Tasmania*, Melbourne, Georgian House, 1970.

—— *Adelaide Lace*, Adelaide, Rigby, 1973.

—— *Carlton*, Adelaide, Rigby, 1974.

—— and Craig, Edith N. *Early Houses of Northern Tasmania; an Historical and Architectural Survey*, Melbourne, Georgian House, 1964.

—— and Robertson, Joan. *Parkville*, Melbourne, Georgian House, 1975.

Royal Australian Institute of Architects, Queensland Chapter. *Buildings of Queensland*, Brisbane, Jacaranda Press, 1959.

Smith, Bernard and Kate. *The Architectural Character of Glebe, Sydney*, Sydney, University Co-operative Bookshop, 1973.

St Luke's Church, 1855–1955, Centenary Booklet, Adelaide, Hunkin, Ellis and King, 1955.

Stephens, William, Excelsior Foundry, South Melbourne. See above, 'Catalogues'.

Stewart & Harley, 'Sun' Foundry, Adelaide. See above, 'Catalogues'.

'Suit for Infringement of Rights in Patterns of Castings', *The Australasian Iron-monger, Builder, Engineer and Metal Worker*, II, no. 4, 1 April 1887, pp. 84–85.

Year Book of Facts in Science and Art (by John Timbs), London, David Bogue, 1855.

Young, Charles D. & Co., Edinburgh. See above, 'Catalogues'.

Empires and Influences

Duff, J. Clarence. *Pen Sketches of Historic Toronto*, Toronto, the author, 1967.

Krakow, H. L. *Early Cast Iron Façades in Montreal*, 1955.

Nilsson, S. *European Architecture in India 1750–1850*, London, Faber and Faber, 1968.

Picton-Seymour, Désirée and Webster, R. I. B. *Western Provincial, an Album of Paintings and Drawings of the Western Cape*, Cape Town, Maskew Miller, 1952.

Index Numbers in *italic* type refer to plates and captions

Figure 15   *The showroom of Walter Macfarlane & Co., Saracen Foundry, Glasgow, from the 6th edition of their catalogue, 1882–83.*